The CAPITAL CAMPAIGN in Higher Education

A Practical Guide for College and University Advancement

G. David Gearhart
Senior Vice President for Development
and University Relations
The Pennsylvania State University

NACUBO

Library of Congress Cataloging-in-Publication Data

Gearhart, G. David
    The capital campaign in higher education : a practical guide
for college and university advancement / G. David Gearhart
        p.   cm.
    ISBN 0-915164-98-1
    1. Educational fund raising—United States. 2. Universities
and colleges—United States—Finance. I. Title
LB2336.G43   1995
378′.02—dc20   94-44547
                                                CIP

© Copyright 1995 by the National Association
of College and University Business Officers
One Dupont Circle
Washington, DC 20036

Edited by Donna Klinger
Designed by Stacey Trey

Contents

Acknowledgments

I would like to express special gratitude to David John Lieb for assisting with the compilation of the research for this book. His diligent efforts were invaluable to the publication of this book, and I am grateful to him for his professional support.

I want to express special thanks to my office staff at The Pennsylvania State University. Sandra Thompson, Jan Oakes, Maggie Crispell, and Barbara Ryzner were extraordinarily patient and helpful as this project moved forward. I also wish to thank Bernadine B. Prince, who was an early inspiration for this book.

Special appreciation is expressed to Martha Bushā for her technical expertise in assisting with the first draft of the manuscript. I am also grateful to Michael Bezilla who assisted in the editing of the book and provided helpful suggestions.

I also wish to acknowledge the fund-raising consulting firm of Grenzebach Glier and Associates, Inc., of Chicago, Illinois. Chairman Martin Grenzebach and President and CEO John Glier have provided their expertise and guidance to me for many years, and much of their "wisdom" is reflected throughout these pages.

Also, I want to express deepest appreciation to the senior staff in the Division of Development and University Relations, Brad Choate, Peter Weiler, Roger Williams, and Barbara Coyle; and key staff in the Office of Development, Bob Groves, Dan Saftig, Jim Rhodes, and Leslie Saftig, who provided encouragement, constructive criticism, and experienced advice during the writing of this book.

Gratitude is expressed to H. Bryce Jordan, 14th president of The Pennsylvania State University, under whose leadership I began this book and to Joab Thomas, 15th president of Penn State, under whose leadership I completed it. I am also grateful to the many volunteers of the university whose inspiration contributed to this project, particularly the chairman of our Board of Trustees, William A. Schreyer, and the chairman of The Penn State National Development Council, Edward R. Hintz.

Finally, I wish to express gratitude to Roy B. Shilling Jr., president of Southwestern University in Georgetown, Texas, who has been an inspiration to me throughout my professional career.

This book is dedicated to my wife, Jane Brockmann Gearhart, and our children, Katy and Brock.

Foreword

Regardless of the label that may be applied to the function of garnering financial resources for institutions of higher learning—fund raising, institutional advancement, or development—there is one thing that is certain: philanthropic support is critically important to any college or university that seeks to be one of the best of its type within the United States. The proliferation of advancement staff has been one of the most dramatic changes in higher education in the last 20 years. Virtually every college or university—public and independent—in America is now involved in some aspect of fund raising. The acute competition for resources is forcing institutions to place a major emphasis on development.

Currently, more than 300 colleges and universities are conducting major capital campaigns, and in the big picture more than one-third of all institutions have mounted a campaign at some time in their recent history. Development personnel have become highly skilled and sought after, as even a casual glance at the classified section of *The Chronicle of Higher Education* will attest. Presidents, governing boards, regents, financial officers, and senior administrators have come to recognize that running a capital campaign requires considerable expertise and a total institutional commitment. These administrators realize that the entire ethos of a college or university is involved in moving an institution forward through a capital campaign, and they know that a successful campaign can fundamentally transform an institution. Entire campuses, colleges, and departments can be galvanized by major philanthropic support. Research initiatives can be bolstered by the infusion of gift support, and renowned faculty who might otherwise be lured away by competing institutions can be convinced to remain with the promise of an endowed position that provides research dollars, clerical support, and extra stipends. Campaign dollars can endow more scholarships to help recruit the best and brightest students. The capital campaign is crucial to any institution that wants to be on, or remain at, the cutting edge of higher education.

One of higher education's ironies is that there are few formal programs available in which to learn how to prepare for or manage a capital campaign. Although the average institution prepares students to become distinguished members of the professoriate, it offers few opportunities in its curricula for those interested in raising—through capital campaigns—the requisite dollars for the institution's continued growth and enhancement. Only a handful of colleges and universities, including Indiana University and The Pennsylvania State University, offer courses that specifically address development. These programs are the exception. As one development director told me early in my career, "Development is not something that you can teach or learn, it is something that you just go out and do!"

In this book, a distinguished university administrator has made an exemplary effort to fill that void. *The Capital Campaign in Higher Education* serves as an excellent "how-to" guide for planning and implementing capital campaigns in today's colleges and universities. Other books have cast a large net and attempted to define a campaign for any philanthropic organization, be it a major public research university or a small community drive. This book does not attempt such a feat, but instead is specific to fund-raising efforts in higher education. It imparts a general working knowledge of the important attributes and characteristics of the capital campaign in colleges and universities and should be required reading for all development officers and senior administrative personnel.

In short, this book will enable you to "go out and do it."

Dr. Roy B. Shilling Jr.
President
Southwestern University
Georgetown, Texas

Preface

This book provides a practical summary of the major elements of planning and conducting capital campaigns for colleges and universities. As tuition rises faster than the Consumer Price Index and legislative appropriations continue to dwindle in state after state, both public and independent institutions are turning to philanthropic support to maintain and strengthen their academic missions. The only way to garner these critical private dollars on a large scale is to establish an efficient and aggressive development program, staffed with dedicated, knowledgeable professionals. It is for these professionals—both veterans as well as beginners—that this book is primarily intended. However, development professionals need to involve all of the administration in a far-reaching campaign—and, accordingly, administrators need to know the institutionwide aspects of a capital campaign. This book, then, also addresses the broader aspects of development, and as such is also for presidents, governing boards, and business officers.

There can be little doubt that capital campaigns are increasingly prominent, and they are likely to gain even more visibility in the future. In fact, they are even becoming prevalent on an international basis. One needs only to cite the recent wave of capital campaigns in the United Kingdom and, in particular, the dramatic success of the Campaign for Oxford.

Indeed, the capital campaign has become so entrenched at colleges and universities that academic administrators, alumni association officers, faculty, and even volunteers and prospective donors are likely to be affected in one way or another at a participating institution. It is for these groups also that this book has been prepared.

The goal of this book is to present practical information in a simple, easy-to-absorb manner. The chapters form a blueprint of the organization, staffing, and implementation of major fund-raising efforts in higher education. Chapter 1 defines the capital campaign and discusses its growth in recent years. It reviews those elements that must be in place at any institution even *before* serious campaign planning begins.

Chapter 2, "Planning for the Campaign," stresses the need to bring an historical perspective to the development program. The chapter then moves into an analysis of the campaign counsel. The campaign case statement and its purposes are reviewed, and the feasibility study is discussed.

Chapter 2 additionally covers the importance of the needs statement of the campaign. The author reviews various theories on the setting of campaign goals, and discusses the negative public reaction mega-campaigns engender, as well as public reaction to public university campaigns and why public institutions need private gift support. Finally, the chapter closes with discussion of the selection of a campaign theme and title.

Chapter 3, "Creating a Campaign Organization," begins with an analysis of the integration of institutional advancement and the proper organization of a development and university relations program.

The chapter addresses the relationship of a capital campaign to ongoing fund-raising activities involving the annual fund, corporate and foundation relations, communications, and the volunteer organization. The roles of the president of the institution, the chief institutional advancement officer, the alumni director, and the university relations or public relations director are outlined in this chapter as well.

Chapter 4 addresses the role of volunteers, and the external organization of the campaign. The recruitment of volunteers; the role of the board of governors; the role of the development council, foundation board, and business office; and the various campaign volunteer committees are scrutinized. The responsibilities of the campaign chairperson, the vice chairpersons, the campaign treasurer, and the campaign liaison are likewise reviewed. The faculty/staff campaign, the student campaign, and the local community campaign as components of the larger effort also are explained. The chapter concludes with a discussion of the alumni association and its duties during the campaign.

Chapter 5 reviews the vitally important *process* of soliciting and asking for the gift. The author presents various theories about why people give or refuse to give to capital campaigns. A short discussion of physicians and attorneys as benefactors is included in this chapter. The issue of prospect management, including the evaluation and rating of prospects, is discussed in Chapter 5.

A look at the process of asking for a gift will take up the bulk of this chapter, which concludes with a study of the common mistakes made in major gift solicitations.

Chapter 6 describes campaign mechanics. This is a "nuts and bolts" chapter that reviews a number of aspects of the campaign, including the recommended percent of the goal to have in hand prior to a public announcement, the cost of a capital campaign, the cost to raise a dollar, the gift range chart, the length of the capital campaign, the frequency of capital campaigns, the campaign timetable, and the campaign pledge form. A brief discussion of campaign cash flow as related to bricks-and-mortar gifts also is a part of chapter 6.

Chapter 7 covers the public relations aspects of the campaign, including precampaign publicity, editorial support, use of internal and external university publications, an advertising plan, use of a speakers bureau, the lead campaign brochure, audio visuals, and donor-recognition events.

Chapter 8 examines campaign accounting and what should be counted in a capital campaign based on national guidelines promulgated by the Council for Advancement and Support of Education (CASE).

Chapter 9 reviews the post-campaign plan and sets an agenda for future institutional fund raising.

O N E

The Capital Campaign: An Overview

In 1991, aproximately $124 billion was given away in the United States,[1] which averages out to more than $100,000 for every minute of every day. Philanthropy is big business—entire marketing firms with huge, specialized staffs monitor the mood swings of Americans in an attempt to secure financial support from large numbers of people for worthy (and not so worthy) causes. These "giving specialists" have made a science of understanding why people are likely to be philanthropic toward one project and not so generous toward the next. This is an important question, as the existence of entire institutions, including social and religious organizations, depends solely on the support of private dollars and the continued benevolence of the American people.

Evidence of philanthropy dates back as far as 4,000 B.C., but as Jon Van Til and Associates point out, the systematic practice of "fund raising" is truly an American tradition.[2]

Nowhere have the philanthropic practices of the American people been more apparent than in higher education. Geiger states, "Private giving has greatly abetted the relative abundance of resources in the diverse institutional orientations that have allowed the American system of higher education to become the most extensive in the world."[3] Even before this nation was founded, philanthropy was evident in all sectors of colonial society. The Ivy League institutions, for example, were built largely on the dreams of wealthy philanthropists who desired to perpetuate their family names by the socially responsible act of giving away their fortunes. Throughout the nineteenth century, great colleges and universities continued to be established by men and women who gave unselfishly of their resources.

The Capital Campaign at Colleges and Universities

A natural outgrowth of the philanthropic presence at colleges and universities is the capital campaign. Capital campaigns, as they exist today, appear to be a 20th century phenomenon.[4] The last few years have seen a virtual explosion of capital campaigns from one campus to the next. Since the early 1980s, more than 100 major American research universities have launched capital campaigns, some with goals as high as $1.5 billion.[5] Many more institutions, both public and independent, are poised to begin campaigns. Indeed, few are the colleges and universities that are not planning or engaged in sizable private fund-raising efforts. To ignore such ventures is to risk being left behind amid intensifying competition.

A common thread that runs through the psyche of the American public is the need to be successful. Bigger, grander, broader, bolder, and better are all adjectives that describe traditional American aspirations. The spirit of competition runs deep in every aspect of our society. Little wonder, then, that the rush to announce so-called mega-campaigns has become an integral part of higher education.

Capital campaigns are now being conducted by hundreds—perhaps thousands—of charities for a diverse range of purposes. Of course, not all of these charitable organizations are academic institutions. In fact, most of the capital campaigns in this country are conducted by nonprofit eleemosynary organizations, and colleges and universities make up only a small fraction of their number. Consider the capital campaigns of such groups as the Boys Club of America, Girl Scouts, Boy Scouts, fraternities, sororities, hospitals, historical societies, orchestras, synagogues, mosques, the American Heart Association, Easter Seals, United Way, Special Olympics, symphonies, churches, temples, the American Cancer Society, and the Muscular Dystrophy Association—the list is endless. Suffice it to say that in 1994, the Internal Revenue Service recognized 1,024,648 tax-exempt organizations—a conservative number to be sure.[6]

In State College, Pennsylvania (home of The Pennsylvania State University's University Park campus), a small borough with a population of 38,000, 24 separate capital campaigns by local organizations were underway in 1994.

Many more kinds of organizations are engaged in capital campaigning today than 10 years ago. Human service groups, public television stations, YMCAs, symphony orchestras, independent secondary schools—and now even primary schools—are all launching capital campaigns. Information about capital campaigns for nursery schools has not been forthcoming, but some no doubt exist.

The 1980s were heady times for higher education institutions. Buoyed by an expanding economy, private giving to colleges and universities grew by 134 percent, from $3.8 billion in 1979–80 to $8.9 billion in 1988–89, according to the Council for Financial Aid to Education (CFAE).[7]

Eight independent research universities (Harvard, Princeton, Yale, Stanford, Columbia, Washington, and Northwestern universities and Massachusetts Institute of Technology) saw their endowments soar through the billion dollar threshold. Four others (Stanford, New York, and Boston universities and the University of Pennsylvania) launched billion-dollar campaigns. In 1991, Columbia University announced a goal of more than $1 billion. Yale launched a campaign with a goal of $1.5 billion, and in 1993 Harvard embarked on the biggest campaign ever, with a stated goal of $2.1 billion.

Public colleges and universities also jumped aggressively into the fund-raising arena during the 1980s. Although lacking a philanthropic tradition as strong as their independent counterparts, five public research universities (the Universities of California at Berkeley, Minnesota, and California at Los Angeles and Ohio State and Pennsylvania State universities) completed campaigns that each raised at least $300 million. In 1992, the University of Michigan launched a $1 billion campaign, the first ever by a public university, although $150 million of the goal consists of will expectancies.

The Capital Campaign—A Definition

What is meant by "capital campaign"? The term is probably one of the most confusing in the higher education fund-raising vocabulary and conjures up all kinds of misconceptions. Capital has been defined by economists as "a produced factor of production."[8] Today's capital campaign, however, has in a sense become a generic term that describes an intense effort to raise funds from the private sector through multiyear pledge commitments within a specified period of time. The capital campaign should really be renamed "a major gifts campaign." No longer are gifts sought only for bricks-and-mortar programs. Now the typical capital campaign at a college or university includes all philanthropy—annual gifts, bricks-and-mortar gifts, endowment gifts, program support gifts, and research funds. Rare is the college or university capital campaign that does not include every gift that is received during the life of that campaign.

A capital campaign essentially positions an institution to publicly proclaim its critical need for private gift support that will allow the continuation of current academic programs as well as the launching of important new initiatives. In a capital campaign the college or university declares that it is serious about philanthropy and that it is bringing together faculty, students, administrators, the governing board, alumni, legislators, friends, and the public at large in an all-out effort to garner private financial support.

Most fund-raising professionals accept this broad definition. Kent E. Dove, for example, describes the capital campaign as "an organized, intensive, fund-raising effort on the part of the third sector institution or organization to secure extraordinary gifts and pledges for a specific purpose or purposes (such as building, construction, renovation, equipment, acquisition, or endowment funds) during a specified period of time." [9]

There are a few hold-outs to be sure. Russell Kohr, for instance, says that using the above description to define a capital campaign is "something of a misnomer." A traditionalist, he believes that a strict definition requires that capital projects are those for additions to plants or endowments.[10] Nevertheless, capital campaign has become the most widely accepted term for systematic, major-gift, time-specific fund raising. This term has weathered the test of time and will continue to be used to describe any major effort with a prescribed time frame seeking financial support from the private sector. Annual giving, planned giving, bricks-and-mortar gifts, endowment gifts, or gifts-in-kind—most institutions wrap all of these under the rubric of capital campaigns.

The capital campaign also is a declaration by the institution that garnering private financial support will be a critical priority, not only in the short term, but in the long term as well.

Institutional Readiness for a Capital Campaign

Priorities at institutions of higher learning swing back and forth like a pendulum. One administration might emphasize student affairs, campus beautification, and faculty initiatives while the next will concentrate on research, the improvement of teaching, and curricular development. It is not possible for a president or chancellor to be all things to all constituencies. He or she must concentrate on selective program thrusts to make substantial progress. Yet there can be no question that securing financial resources from the private sector must be one of the highest priorities of any administration, regardless of other thrusts. One need only look at a few institutions that have recently moved into the forefront of American higher education, in large measure because of the philanthropic support they have secured.

A few years ago, Southwestern University, in Georgetown, Texas, was a small-town, small-time college fairly well regarded in Texas, but not even well known outside of a three- or four-state area. In a matter of a few years, a new president transformed it into one of America's outstanding independent liberal arts colleges through a combination of inspired leadership and massive private financial support. Today, Southwestern University has one of the largest endowments per student of any college or university in the nation.[11]

The transformation that has taken place at Emory University after the $105 million gift from Robert W. Woodruff in 1979 is equally impressive. The Woodruff gift, combined with several others, has placed Emory in a competitive position with many Ivy League institutions. Emory regularly raids some of the top independent universities in the country for renowned faculty.

The case of Rice University in Houston, Texas, is also noteworthy. Generous Texas Foundation resources, coupled with philanthropy from alumni and friends, have transformed Rice into one of the best institutions—public or independent—in the United States. A little-known institution 10 years ago, Rice is now attracting some of the best and brightest students in America. It has been able to secure a nationally recognized faculty and has assembled some of the keenest thinkers from throughout the world. [12]

All of these institutions, as diverse as they may be, share the blessings of major philanthropy. Each has had whole departments transformed through corporate, foundation, individual, and alumni support. Each has moved forward dramatically because of bold leadership, but also—more importantly—because of private philanthropy. They have clearly demonstrated that private giving can and will substantially change the course of an institution for the better.

However, many institutions are not positioned to increase private support by launching a capital campaign.

When considering a major capital campaign, the following questions must be addressed:

1. **Is the Chief Executive Officer of the Institution Committed to a Capital Campaign?**

   Without a doubt, the person who is crucial to the success of a capital campaign is the president of the institution. Without his or her total backing, success will be a struggle. As G.T. Smith states, "Success in institutional advancement depends ultimately on the chief executive and that officer's willingness and capacity for leadership in the advancement effort." [13] This commitment cannot be lip service. Not only must the president wholeheartedly accept and welcome a major gifts campaign, but he or she must be prepared to be the principal spokesperson. The president must be willing to speak to faculty, deans, students, alumni—all of the constituents of the institution—and indicate that the campaign is an absolute top priority. The president must accept the fact that he or she must spend a predominant amount of time over the coming years to see the campaign through to fruition.

   In addition, the president must appreciate what it takes to run a capital campaign. New resources, new staff, and an overall commitment by the entire college or university will be required for success. The president must be at the forefront, pushing, prodding, and diligent in his or her quest for financial support. Without the president's leadership, the capital campaign will wither. It will never become an institutional priority, and will ultimately die from lack of interest.

2. Is There Leadership from the Governing Body?

The governing board, board of regents, or other governing body of the institution must acknowledge that the capital campaign will be the most important event at the institution for the next several years. Nothing else can take precedence. The governing board must unmistakably signal that the campaign has top institutional priority and must back the president fully in pursuing the philanthropic goal.[14]

Members of the governing board also must commit their own resources, time, and talent to the campaign. Many development officers at public universities might dispute this point, arguing that many board members are political appointees who secured their seats as part of a political payback, and who simply know the governor or are a member of the party that happens to be in power in the statehouse.

Admittedly, many public university governing board members—political appointees included—do not have the financial ability to make major commitments to a capital campaign. Yet all of them, regardless of financial resources, do have the ability to participate at some level. Their participation will be crucial to the success of the campaign. As Kent E. Dove states:

> Without the board's visible and unanimous commitment, it will be difficult if not impossible to motivate others to participate. And it is the governing board members, independent of others, who must eventually commit themselves to seeing that a stated goal is reached because they themselves are unanimously determined that it will be.[15]

Early on in a campaign, members of the governing board should be asked to verify the effort through a board resolution. This resolution should give the president the authority to carry out the program and should back the campaign completely. An example of this issue was never more evident than a 1992 report by *The Chronicle of Higher Education* stating that the president of Rice University had resigned his position because of lack of support by the governing board for a new capital campaign. This was a bit ironic, given Rice's outstanding success in transforming the institution through private philanthropy.[16]

3. **Is There a Committed Professional Staff in Place?**

An institution is far from ready for a capital campaign if it does not have a dedicated professional staff that understands the importance of development in higher education. This does not necessarily mean that the chief development officer must be a seasoned veteran of previous campaigns. Many campaigns are run by people who are in their first such effort and who are relative novices at capital campaigning.

On the other hand, the development staff should most definitely have some experience in higher education fund raising and should be willing to tap into other resources—a fund-raising consulting firm, for example—to gain the necessary leadership expertise.

No matter how many staff members the campaign requires, the principal players must be willing to see the campaign through to completion. They should sign on for the life of the campaign. Many colleges and universities lose the chief development officer two or three years into a five- or six-year capital campaign. Often, the chief development officer is lured away by another institution with the promise of increased salary and perquisites. Wise institutions ensure staff stability through a contractual arrangement that gives the senior staff member a stable environment.

Equally important are the employees who report to the chief development officer. Continuity in the campaign office is vital, and those signing on to a capital campaign should give assurances to their supervisor that they will see the campaign through to its conclusion. Changes in key staff positions can have a debilitating impact on the campaign, and staff stability should be an important priority when organizing and implementing a campaign.

4. **Are Senior Officers Supportive?**

It is not enough that the president is totally committed to a capital campaign, even though that is the most important element in judging the internal readiness of an institution to start campaign planning. Other senior officers must be equally as committed and supportive before planning can begin. The *chief financial officer* is one of the key senior officers. In most institutions, he or she controls vast resources, staff, personnel, and institutional operations. A chief financial officer who does not believe in the worth of private giving, much less a capital campaign, can make the life of the chief development officer miserable, and derail the campaign. According to Carroll Rickert, ". . . the efforts of both financial and development officers, and their ability to serve the institution, are enhanced by their working together."[17]

Activities such as timely acknowledgment of gifts, valuation of securities, determining principal amounts required for endowments, personnel policies for hiring appropriate development staff, and advance funds for preliminary campaigning can all be under the control of the chief financial officer, and are crucial considerations on any campus. Therefore, this person must be a part of the planning and implementation of the capital campaign from its very beginning. He or she must be made an integral part of every aspect of the campaign, and an important partnership between the chief development officer and the chief financial officer must be forged.

This is sometimes difficult to accomplish. After all, the chief financial officer has many responsibilities, and the implementation of a capital campaign is, in some ways, outside of his or her normal operations. Drawing the chief financial officer into discussions about the campaign can require effort. However, that officer can open doors that no one else—including the president—can open as quickly and as efficiently, and a good working relationship between the business office and the campaign office will make life much easier in the initial stages of the campaign. The fiscal officer must be one of the "owners" of the campaign, and this can only be accomplished by involving that person from the very outset of the effort. A prudent financial officer will realize the importance of the campaign and will seek to be involved at the earliest opportunity.

Another important party is the *chief academic officer.* Because the development function at a college or university is a relatively new phenomenon in higher education, many faculty and academicians will be skeptical about any program that is forthcoming from the development office. A major multipurpose campaign that proposes to include faculty, staff, students, and alumni will be given very close scrutiny by the academic leadership. William Pickett writes:

> In academic organizations, the faculty are the ultimate decision makers. In institutions where the most important activity is teachers teaching and students learning, the decisions of individual faculty members have the most powerful impact on the quality and the success of that endeavor. Faculty members must be at the center of the long-range planning process.[18]

Consequently, the early involvement of the chief academic officer in planning the campaign will help to avoid any misconceptions about the purposes and thrust of the effort. A good chief academic officer can be invaluable in smoothing any academic feathers that might be ruffled when the campaign is vigorously underway. In addition, this officer must take the lead along with the president to determine those critical priorities that will be targeted to receive financial support.

As will be seen later, the formation of a "needs statement" should be the sole prerogative of the academic leadership of the college or university, and the academic officer must be the catalyst that ultimately brings together divergent interests into a solid, cohesive, systematic plan that includes all of the projects that the campaign will seek to fund. Do not allow the chief academic officer to be on the outside of the campaign planning. Make the officer an integral force from the beginning. This is not always easy as there tends to be a natural tug of war between external relations personnel and academic leadership. Do not allow friction to develop; keep lines of communication open throughout the life of a campaign.

5. **Is There a Supportive Constituency?**
An institution's primary external volunteer constituents must be generally supportive of the need to begin the process of planning the capital campaign. Alumni volunteers who support the need for a strong development program and are willing to give time, talent, and resources are invaluable to the process. The issue here is the direct support and personal involvement of a group of volunteer leaders who spark interest

and support from other alumni leaders. The feasibility of major gifts from constituents is addressed in chapter 2.

The main point concerning the parties involved is to bring them in as early as possible in the campaign. Make them feel included, and the campaign has a much better chance for success.

Keep in mind that a capital campaign is not the sole province of the development staff. The development staff, even though intimately involved in every detail of the campaign, should be considered facilitators and implementors. Without the board of governors, the president, and the chief officers of the institution behind the campaign, it will not be a successful effort. *It is not the development office's campaign.* It is the college or university's campaign, and the backing of the entire institution must be evident from the beginning of the effort.

If the president of the institution is solidly behind the concept of a campaign—not just in name, but in vigorously promoting and supporting the concept—then the institution is one essential step closer to *beginning planning.* If the governing board has shown support and enthusiasm for the concept, then the institution is a second step *closer to planning.* If the institution has a cohesive development office with vigorous and visible leadership that plans to remain a part of the institution for the foreseeable future, then this fortunate institution is three steps closer to *planning for a campaign.* If the senior officers support the concept fully and are willing to devote their time and the institution's resources to planning and promoting the campaign, and if a small but vigorous alumni volunteer group will take a leadership role, then it would appear the institution is now ready to begin the first phase of *planning* toward a capital campaign. Note the emphasis is still on planning. By no means should the institution precipitously launch an effort. All that has been determined is that the *internal audiences* that will be absolutely critical to the success of the campaign are in favor of beginning the planning stages. Whether the institution is ultimately in a position to launch the effort will require further study. However, discussions, internally and on a limited basis, can now begin.

Notes

1. Ann E. Kaplan, ed., *Giving USA: The Annual Report on Philanthropy for the Year 1991.* (Joanne Hayes Publisher), p. 10.
2. Jon Van Til and Associates, *Critical Issues in American Philanthropy: Strengthening Theory and Practice.* (San Francisco: Jossey-Bass Inc., 1990), pp. 4, 13.
3. Roger Geiger, Foreword, in Jesse Brundage Sears, *Philanthropy in the History of American Higher Education.* (New Brunswick, NJ: Transaction Publishers, 1990), p. xiv.
4. Kent E. Dove, *Conducting a Successful Capital Campaign: A Comprehensive Guide for Nonprofit Organizations.* (San Francisco: Jossey-Bass Inc., 1988), p. 3.
5. Brakeley, John Price Jones, Inc., *Capital Campaign Report.* (Stamford, CT: Brakeley, John Price Jones, Inc., Spring 1992).
6. Virginia Ann Hodgkinson, Murray S. Weitzman, Christopher M. Toppe, Stephen M. Noga, Internal Revenue Service Annual Report, Various Editions in Nonprofit Almanac 1992–1993 (San Francisco: Jossey Bass, Inc.).
7. Council for Financial Aid to Education, *Voluntary Support of Education 1979–80 and 1988–89.* (New York: Council for Financial Aid to Education, 1981 and 1990).
8. Paul A. Samuelson, W. D. Norhaus, *Economics.* (New York: McGraw-Hill, 1989), p. 50.
9. Dove, *Conducting a Successful Capital Campaign: A Comprehensive Guide for Nonprofit Organizations,* p. 1.
10. Russell V. Kohr, "Capital Campaigns," in A. Westley Rowland, ed., *Handbook of Institutional Advancement: A Practical Guide to College and University Relations, Fund Raising, Alumni Relations, Government Relations, Publications, and Executive Management for Continued Advancement* (San Francisco: Jossey-Bass Inc., 1977), p. 237.
11. The Chronicle of Higher Education, *The Chronicle of Higher Education Almanac vol. xxxix no. 1:* (August 26, 1992): 35.
12. James Cass, M. Birnbaum, *Comparative Guide to American Colleges: For Students, Parents, and Counselors 15th ed.* (New York: Harper Perennial, 1991), pp. 493–494.
13. G. T. Smith, "The Chief Executive and Advancement," in A. Westley Rowland, ed., *Handbook of Institutional Advancement: A Modern Guide to Executive Management, Institutional Relations,*

Fund-Raising, Alumni Administration, Government Relations, Publications, Periodicals and Enrollment Management (San Francisco: Jossey-Bass Inc., 1986), p. 697.

14. Robert L. Krit, *The Fund-Raising Handbook.* (The United States of America: Scott Foresman Professional Books, 1991), p. 54.
15. Dove, *Conducting a Successful Capital Campaign: A Comprehensive Guide for Nonprofit Organizations*, p. 32.
16. Michael Cinell, "Duncan Discusses Rice After Rupp," in *Rice News Vol 2, No.11*: (October 29, 1992): 1, 4.
17. Carroll Rickert, "The Business Officer as an Ally and Associate," in Francis Pray, *Handbook for Educational Fund Raising: A Guide to Successful Principles and Practices for Colleges, Universities and Schools* 2nd ed. (San Francisco: Jossey-Bass Inc., 1981), p. 193.
18. William Pickett, "The Long-Range Planning Process," in H. Quigg, ed., *The Successful Capital Campaign: From Planning to Victory Celebration*, (Washington, DC: Council for the Advancement and Support of Education, 1986), pp. 8, 9.

TWO

Planning for the Campaign

C hapter 1 set the stage for a college or university to begin contemplating a major capital campaign. After convincing internal officers that a campaign is in the best interests of the institution and including key volunteers in the discussion process, it is time to begin vigorous planning toward a capital campaign.

At many institutions, planning for a capital campaign never ceases. This is particularly true at those institutions that have become experienced fund raisers over the last 25 years. Before a campaign has ceased operation and the final date of campaign counting has even arrived, development officials are already planning for the next (inevitable) major fund-raising effort. Robert L. Krit submits that to properly prepare for a capital campaign, an institution should begin planning at least *one year* before the start of the campaign.[1] This planning is oftentimes conducted quietly among college and university officials, but the thought processes centered around timing, major gift prospects, and institutional readiness are already in place. Of all the important elements in a capital campaign, and there are many, planning must head the list.

Creating a Historical Perspective—Beginning the Planning Process

Development staff should create a written document that outlines the program in detail from a historical perspective. An institution cannot possibly look to the future without knowing its past. Knowledge of an institution's ability to raise major gifts is essential. Is there a history of strong major gift fund raising at the institution? Has it been successful in garnering financial support for smaller capital projects? Has the annual fund program produced steady support for academic efforts? Answers to these questions will help establish realistic campaign boundaries.

Development officers should consider reviewing total gift support for the past 10 years, examining their institution's ability to progress incrementally from year to year in its development program. It would be unwise to push for a capital campaign with no historical base of support from which to draw. History is replete with colleges and universities and other philanthropic organizations and agencies that "intuitively" believe they can launch a major capital campaign without appreciating the importance of an ongoing effort that provides a base of support and a pool of volunteers. As Kent E. Dove states in his book, *Conducting a Successful Capital Campaign*,

> Realism is necessary in determining capital campaign goals or, indeed, whether an institution is even ready to enter into a capital campaign . . . Past performance as well as current trends in giving must be analyzed. An institution annually raising $500,000 is not likely to be prepared to mount a successful campaign for $30 million.[2]

A historical perspective can be easily accomplished by producing a three- to five-page document that will establish historical parameters.

Campaign Counsel

Consider employing campaign counsel early in the planning stages, rather than asking counsel to join the team after key decisions have been made. Campaign counsel may find it difficult to operate under preexisting campaign guidelines, particularly if there is disagreement with major organizational issues.

The decision to employ campaign counsel is always a difficult one. Many development officers believe hiring campaign counsel is a "necessary evil" and that counsel can provide a different dimension and perspective when working to establish policies and procedures early in campaign planning.[3]

The employment of campaign counsel is not an inexpensive proposition. Currently, most of the larger, more established firms charge between $1,000 and $2,500 a day plus expenses, although senior officers at a few firms charge more. Fees are generally negotiable and depend greatly on the level of expertise and experience of the counsel assigned to an institution.

How does one determine if counsel is necessary or desirable? A checklist is provided in figure 2.1.

Figure 2.1 Determining the Necessity of Counsel

An institution may benefit from employing campaign counsel if:

1. Development staff has limited experience in capital campaigning. Counsel can help to fill that void.
2. The institution has limited resources and cannot hire, as chief development officer, a seasoned development professional with solid campaign experience. Counsel can "bring to the table" the necessary knowledge and ability to move a campaign forward.
3. The president and senior officers of the institution are supporting the capital campaign but not vigorously. Campaign counsel often can help shape the president's opinion about the need for additional resources for the campaign and can provide "political muscle" to convince college and university leadership of the need for new resources, additional staff, and commitment of presidential time.
4. Senior development staff members need help verifying their management and organizational decisions. The employment of campaign counsel brings a new and different perspective that can augment the opinions of internal development staff.
5. Development staff could benefit from knowledge of "cutting-edge" development initiatives at other institutions. Although it is inappropriate for counsel to share confidential information about other institutions' capital campaigns, general knowledge about new initiatives can be most helpful to campaign planning.
6. Assistance is needed in motivating volunteers and giving them a sense of professionalism. The "comfort level" of volunteers can increase dramatically if they have faith in counsel and believe the campaign is being organized in the best professional manner.
7. The institution could benefit from project-specific expertise that counsel can provide for a variety of campaign efforts. Often

---

Figure 2.1 (Continued)

institutions will employ campaign counsel for specific projects such as conducting a feasibility study, publishing the lead brochure, producing a video for use by staff and volunteers, or providing technical planned giving and tax advice for complex major gifts. Having counsel handle these tasks can save valuable time for development officers who are concentrating on the cultivation and solicitation of major gift prospects.

8. A sounding board is needed for professional staff who may not communicate their needs and ideas to senior development officials or senior officers of the institution. Counsel, when appropriate, can be "brokers of information" and assist in solving problems internally among staff members with competing priorities.

9. The most senior development officer of the institution needs a sounding board for confidential campaign problems, particularly in the area of personnel decisions. Campaign counsel can serve as a confidant who is connected to the campaign and is in the inner circle of campaign planning, but is not a direct member of the senior officer's staff.

Selecting the best firm can be a difficult and time-consuming process. However, development staff and senior administrators must devote adequate time and resources to it. Choosing counsel with the "proper fit" is important for early success in the campaign.[4]

When selecting campaign counsel, consider the guidelines presented in figure 2.2.

When considering counsel, keep in mind that it is not always necessary to choose a large, well-established firm. With increasing frequency, institutions are choosing chief development officers at other institutions to serve as campaign counsel.

As H. Russell Bintzer pointed out more than 10 years ago,

Almost all [independent counselors] have one characteristic in common: a background of successful service in one or another educational or health-related institution. Most of these 'independents' serve a particular level of institution or a particular part of the country. They rely heavily on word-of-mouth advertising to acquire new clients, and almost all work for lower fees and costs than do the members of the American Association of Fund Raising Counsel.[5]

Figure 2.2   Guidelines for Selecting Campaign Counsel

1. Conducting personal interviews with several firms is a prerequisite when choosing campaign counsel. Both the chief executive officer *and* the specific individual who will be assigned to the campaign should come to campus for an extensive interview with appropriate administrators. Prospective campaign counsel and the chief executive officer of the firm should plan to meet with the president of the institution, senior development officer, senior officers of the institution, and major volunteer leadership. At some institutions it is appropriate for campaign counsel to have some exposure to members of the governing board. Most good firms will request exposure to these groups, but campaign staff should seek wide concurrence among internal and external groups before employing campaign counsel.

2. Interview a minimum of three firms before making a decision on campaign counsel. Choose firms with different staff sizes to gain the broadest perspective possible.

3. Confidential discussions with other senior development personnel at other institutions that have employed counsel is important prior to the firm's visit to campus. Generally, development staff members are eager to critique campaign counsel, and it is a good way to gain a perspective on a firm prior to agreeing to a visit.

4. Tell the firm that it must make a case for why it should be chosen. The firm must explain what they will do to help ensure the success of the campaign.

5. Ask the firm to list successful campaigns for which it has provided counsel, and to include specific names of development officers with whom members have worked. Contact the references they provide, but also interview others who were not selected.

6. After the delegates have visited the institution, ask the firm to provide a brief written document containing observations about the upcoming campaign. The firms that are eager for the business will follow up quickly and efficiently, and the document will also provide an opportunity to review the firm's ability to learn quickly after observing the key players at the institution.

7. Check the background and require the vita of the individual who will be assigned to the institution, and investigate that vita carefully to verify pertinent information. Interview individuals who know the person assigned to the institution to be certain that his or her experience is adequate to provide the assistance and direction that is expected during the campaign.

Many of these officers, generally at the vice president level, are allowed by their respective presidents to serve as campaign counsel on a selective and limited basis. Most will have solid campaign track records with years of experience in development programs. Often these individuals can provide one to three days a month of campaign consultation and bring a practical perspective to the position of campaign counsel. These individuals have enjoyed success in their professional positions and are knowledgeable of every aspect of campaign organization. Many times their fees are much less than the fees of major firms as overhead costs can be kept to a minimum.

An important question to be decided prior to interviewing a firm is the projected length of service, as well as the number of days the firm will devote to the campaign.

Here are some guidelines:

1. Larger campaign counsel firms will argue for the placement of a full-time senior member of the firm on campus to provide day-to-day advice and assistance to campaign staff. Be wary of committing to full-time counsel. Not only can this be extraordinarily expensive (more than $200,000 per year in some cases), but it may mean delegating management issues to counsel that should be reserved for permanent senior development personnel. It is difficult for full-time counsel to do anything less than guide, direct, and manage the total capital campaign for an institution, and senior development staff should be prepared to abdicate responsibility in some areas to campaign counsel if counsel has been established on-site in a full-time capacity. Employ full-time counsel only in extraordinary cases where very little or no campaign experience exists among development staff. An institution would be better served by hiring a person at the vice president level with thorough campaign experience.

2. Generally, spending two to three days per month with campaign counsel is sufficient. These sessions should be highly structured, with definitive agendas distributed in advance of the counsel's visit. Verifiable objectives should be determined in advance so that counsel is aware of what needs to be accomplished during that visit. Longer terms of one or two weeks might be necessary and desirable at the onset of the campaign cycle, but senior development staff will find it difficult to ap-

propriate adequate time for these longer sessions, as they are involved in a plethora of other duties and responsibilities.

3. In many cases, project-specific work—drafting documents, for example—can be carried out at the counsel's office rather than at the institution. A contractual arrangement should allow for this to save travel expenses.

In working with campaign counsel, there are several important general considerations:

1. Counsel should be required to execute a contract with the employing institution. A firm with a good track record will insist on such a document, and the institution, likewise, should insist on formalizing the relationship through a contractual arrangement. The contract should establish the terms of the relationship and the number of days per month that the firm will expend for the institution. Billing procedures, expectation of payment, and ability to cancel the contract should be spelled out for both parties.

   Be sure to provide a clause that requires the firm to seek prior approval of any secondary relationships with institutions within the same geographic region of the college or university. It behooves campaign counsel to contract with multiple institutions in the same geographic region, but an institution should prohibit such conduct if it poses a definite conflict of interest. As an example, it would not appear to be appropriate for campaign counsel to serve two comparable institutions of higher education in the same city or town. Likewise, counsel should not provide services to institutions in the same locale that are in definite competition for funds, students, and faculty. Most campaign counsel contracts do not address this issue. An institution should carefully discuss this potential conflict of interest and include appropriate language in the agreement.

2. Some firms will employ the chief development officer of the institution where they are providing counsel as counsel to other institutions. This is particularly prevalent among major research universities, and it is a practice that should be reviewed very closely. Not only is it a potential conflict of interest, but it smacks of kickbacks and collusion, aspersions that can damage the reputation of the professional as well as the firm. An institution's

president should be fully informed and cognizant of the establishment of any relationship of this type.

3. Often campaign counsel will want to establish a close working relationship with an institution's chief executive officer. It should be made clear from the outset that campaign counsel works for the chief development officer, not the chief executive officer. An institution should have faith in its development officer as the primary contact with campaign counsel. If a president has lost confidence in his or her chief development officer and brings in campaign counsel to help manage this loss of confidence, then development staff should be fully informed of this relationship.

   A few firms have been known to create a conflict between the chief executive officer and the chief development officer, resulting in loss of faith on both sides. Campaign counsel should be providing the fund-raising staff with ongoing advice and expertise, not the president of the institution. If a president seeks his or her own campaign counsel, then it is very likely that the president has lost faith in the institution's entire development program.

4. Campaign counsel may attempt to manage and direct staff even if counsel visits the institution only two or three days a month. There is a natural tendency for the counsel to want to provide hands-on management of the day-to-day operations, but this should be resisted. Campaign counsel should be viewed as just that—counsel. Orders and direction must be reserved for senior development professionals at the institution, and they cannot abdicate their responsibility.

On the plus side, campaign counsel can provide an extraordinary level of expertise. However, the campaign should not be turned over for the exclusive management of counsel, and counsel activities should be monitored on a regular basis. Smaller colleges and universities with less financial resources will find it difficult to employ counsel on a continuous basis. The benefits of counsel expertise, however, may far outweigh the expense involved.

The Campaign Case Statement

Creation of the case statement early on in campaign planning is important. The case statement is an internal document outlining the history of the institution, its mission, and its long- and short-range academic plans as recommended by the president and academic leadership. The case statement presents a basic rationale for the campaign and details the reasons why an institution should move forward with the effort.[6]

There is no particular length requirement for the case statement, and at some institutions a document of four or five pages will suffice. The case statement is primarily an internal document, not necessarily used for a wide audience beyond major volunteers. It is addressed to governing boards, faculty, deans, and key alumni, and describes the thinking of the institution with regard to its mission and the resources required to reach campaign goals.[7] Separate proposals and brochures for individual projects can be derived from the case statement, which also usually forms the core of the central campaign brochure.

Before the document will be used to recruit volunteer leadership, it is important to have it finalized. Figure 2.3 presents the elements of the campaign case statement.

It is not necessary to describe every element of the campaign, as that is the purpose of the institution's needs statement (discussed later). Instead, the case statement outlines these needs in general terms.

The campaign case statement can range from a simple typed document to an elegant, full-color booklet. Whatever form is chosen, it is an important document that should be created early in campaign planning.

The Feasibility Study

The feasibility study is a systematic process undertaken to determine the readiness of an institution to launch a capital campaign. It uses face-to-face interviews with the institution's most important benefactors. It also includes a questionnaire that attempts to determine if an individual prospect is ready and willing to be solicited for a major commitment to the institution. As Allen writes, "The feasibility study is a market survey that tells you how

---

Figure 2.3   The Elements of a Case Statement

A case statement is comprised of the following elements:

1.   A statement of the academic goals and mission of the institution.
2.   A statement linking the goals and mission with the need to provide resources that will enable goals and mission to be achieved.
3.   A statement describing the major areas that have been identified as critically important priorities for funding. In other words, what are the general areas for which the campaign will seek funds? These areas usually include faculty resources, such as endowed chairs, endowed professorships, faculty fellowships, teaching research awards, and other endowment needs; student aid resources, including graduate fellowships and undergraduate scholarships; program resources for instruction, research, or public service; library resources for the augmentation of collections and the acquisition of rare and unique books and journals; capital resources for the construction of new facilities as well as the expansion and modernization of existing facilities; and finally, annual support enhancement, which includes funds for normal growth of the annual fund during the life of the campaign.

---

close your key volunteers and prospects are to full commitment. Unless they are fully informed, fully involved, and fully committed, they will not make their best effort for the upcoming capital campaign."[8]

Once considered an essential element of a capital campaign, the feasibility study is increasingly falling into disuse. This is unfortunate because when conducted properly, it can be the single most important element in the decision to launch a capital campaign. [9]

Feasibility studies are generally conducted by outside counsel. Prospective donors should be made to feel comfortable in sharing confidential information, and prospects are not always willing to do this with development staff. Outside counsel can more convincingly assure prospects that certain sensitive information will remain confidential.

A feasibility study begins with a carefully crafted questionnaire, a sample of which is contained in appendix A and is adapted with the permission of the Grenzebach Glier consulting firm of Chicago. The questionnaire is designed to determine the interest level of a particular prospect in the campaign. The interviewer poses a series of questions, concluding by asking the prospect if he or she would be willing to entertain a commitment to the capital campaign should the institution decide to move forward with the effort. The questionnaire also includes questions about the level of that commitment. The prospect is assured that statements made during the interview will be kept strictly confidential and that the answers to the various questions will not be turned over to the university. Prospective donors can then feel secure about discussing, frankly and honestly, their interest in and ability to contribute to a campaign.

An institution should take care in selecting those individuals to be interviewed. They should be the highest-level prospects available. At least 50 to 75 prospects should be interviewed so that a broad range of information can be obtained. The interviewer then compiles the survey and interview results and presents a detailed document to the institution that generally includes a recommendation as to whether or not the institution should move forward with a capital campaign, based on the anticipated level of major gift support. The interviewer builds his or her recommendations wholly on the interviews.

Often the feasibility study will not necessarily recommend a campaign but will lay out a set of objectives that should be addressed before a campaign is feasible.

There are other kinds of feasibility studies in addition to the standard type described above. These are described below.

Public Feasibility Study

Some institutions have begun using large group meetings where potential benefactors, volunteers, and interested alumni and friends are questioned in a group setting about their interest in and support for a major campaign. Although this method is highly unscientific, it can yield valuable information about institutional readiness and potential for campaign support. It is not recommended as a reliable process to determine the goal of a campaign, however.

Telephone Feasibility Study

Some institutions have begun using the telephone to conduct the feasibility study and question a much broader audience. The advantages to this method are that a large sampling of alumni, friends, and benefactors can be contacted, and much more data can be accumulated and then processed by the interviewer. However, the reliability of the answers to the questions may be suspect given the informality of this medium, calling into question the overall reliability of the study. For smaller projects that don't require a multitude of major gifts, this form might be useful. Face-to-face interviews are still best, particularly when dealing with major gift prospects and current benefactors.

Mail Feasibility Study

Some institutions have mailed questionnaires to alumni regarding their interest in a capital campaign. This can, in many instances, be the most reliable way to accumulate data and does offer the benefit of a much larger sampling than other forms of feasibility studies. However, the likelihood of major gift benefactors completing voluminous forms about fund raising is practically nil. This form of feasibility study is not recommended for a major capital campaign but could potentially be used for a smaller, more focused effort.

Volunteer Feasibility Study

The use of volunteers to conduct the feasibility study is another method that might be considered. In this method, volunteers are assigned to question other volunteers about their interest in a proposed capital campaign and to determine the level of support that might be forthcoming from the volunteer. It is a peer-to-peer study designed to promote support among an institution's constituencies. This method should not be used for goal setting.

Finally, it is important to state again that no institution should move forward vigorously on a capital campaign unless a feasibility study has been conducted and a final report delivered. There simply is no other mechanism to ensure that major gift support will be forthcoming in a campaign. Without the feasibility study, institutions are likely to stumble along the way, after it is too late to change course. The feasibility study should remain an important and essential element to any major capital campaign.[10]

Institutional Strategic Planning and the Needs Statement

The office of development is charged with the responsibility of gathering financial resources to meet the needs that are most critical to the academic enterprise. Directors of development do not determine the listing of needs in a capital campaign. That would be inappropriate as it would place the burden of managing the institution's resources on the development staff. The needs in a capital campaign should be determined, after careful strategic planning, by the academic leadership. The development staff should be involved only in assessing the likelihood of success in meeting these needs.[11]

The president and the chief academic officer should participate in every aspect of determining the needs of the campaign. In large multicampus research universities, the creation of the needs statement can take many months of work, with input from literally hundreds of academic officials. Each department and campus of a major institution should develop a needs statement as an outgrowth of strategic planning. The needs statement must reflect the most important and critical priorities of the institution and must be designed to bring the institution to new heights of academic achievement. When a campaign has been completed and the predominant needs items addressed through philanthropic support, there should be a clear sense that the institution has improved across the board. The needs of the campaign must be the needs of the university, and there must be heavy input from departmental-level faculty, deans, and other academic officials.

The typical call for a listing of academic needs across the institution will produce a list far and above what is practical to fund in a capital campaign. Again, it is the academic leadership of the institution, the president and the chief academic officer, that must finally determine what will be targeted by the campaign's needs statement. This is a difficult process, requiring intimate knowledge of the strategic plan for every unit of the institution.

In small institutions the needs statement may even extend to the departmental level, but should also reflect input from faculty. The needs statement of a small institution may be more reflective of the general needs of the college or university.

Typically, in a major capital campaign, only 60 to 70 percent of the needs statement is ever actually funded. This is not to say that the dollar goal of the campaign will not be met, but the needs statement goal is rarely achieved in its entirety.

A needs statement also should be considered a fluid document that can be changed if necessary throughout the life of the campaign. The chief academic officer should be charged with the responsibility of approving changes to the needs statement. Changes should be made only if there have been curricular and program changes that would make a needs statement item obsolete.

Unlike the case statement, the needs statement should be as specific as possible and should outline, in detail, the desired number of endowments to be created during the campaign, as well as the bricks-and-mortar projects and other needs statement items to be funded from campaign proceeds. Sample needs statements can be found in appendix B. In a major university, each academic unit should outline its needs statement succinctly, indicating the desired number of endowed chairs, endowed professorships, scholarships, and other endowed funds. When possible, these funds should be earmarked for particular departments, so that the development staff is aware of exactly where endowed funds should be placed. Sample language describing endowed funds, building projects, and other important needs can be placed in the needs statement but most definitely should also appear in other campaign literature, such as the lead campaign brochure (see appendix C).

The needs statement becomes the guide for prioritizing activities by the development staff. Development officers should not deviate from the statement when attempting to seek support from benefactors. At any given moment during the campaign, the development staff, along with volunteers, should be seeking support for only those items that are listed on the campaign needs statement. This will keep development officers focused on the major campaign objectives and will not allow faculty and staff with separate agendas to deter funding from a needs statement project or program. The needs statement also should be used to monitor the progress of the campaign to determine if the institution is simply raising funds and "running up numbers" or actually funding the highest priorities of the institution as determined by the strategic planning process and academic leadership.

The needs statement should be released publicly in some form, either as part of the general campaign brochure or printed separately by academic unit. It is not necessary to keep needs statement items confidential, and copies of the statement should be widely distributed so that all internal as well as external audiences are aware of the major items to be funded. Some institutions have used desktop publishing for their needs lists so that they can be easily revised throughout the campaign.

Setting the Goal for the Campaign

Determining the actual monetary target of the campaign can be one of the most difficult processes in the campaign. Too often development staff and volunteers have no idea how to go about setting the goal. They arrive at a dollar figure that has been determined haphazardly and with no sense as to what is realistically possible from their institution's constituencies.

Most campaigns use one of four different goal-setting theories:

Goal Determined by Competing Institutions

Under this theory, a goal is set at a particular level because an institution of similar scope and size is currently operating with that goal. In other words, Institution A is in direct competition with Institution B and believes its goal for the capital campaign must be at least as high as Institution B to avoid public criticism. This "keeping up with the Joneses" philosophy has no basis in scientific data and simply chooses a figure that might be right for one institution but wrong for another institution. It is a sophomoric approach and can create major problems with goal attainment.

Goal Determined by the Needs

This theory simply adds up all of the needs of the institution and arrives at the goal based upon the total aggregate of needs. This is neither a practical nor a politically wise approach and can set a goal much higher than can realistically be attained. The needs statement should be kept totally separate when determining the final dollar goal of a campaign. There is never any correlation between the needs of an institution and the ability to fund those needs. The original needs statement of The Campaign for Penn State totaled more than $900 million, an impossible feat to achieve at the time, given past fund-raising history. The final needs statement was $200 million, later increased to $300 million.

Setting the Goal for Public Relations Purposes

Many institutions set their goal because it has a particular ring to it from a public relations standpoint. Many years ago, there was a rush to be the first institution to declare a capital campaign of more than $100 million. That figure sounded awesome in those days, and a goal was set simply because the figure was impressive to the public at large. More recently, there was a rush to announce billion dollar goals. Again, this theory ignores the basic premise that a goal should be directly related to the number of major gift prospects available.

Goal Determined by Feasibility Study

This is really the only practical and accurate way to determine the goal of a capital campaign. A properly conducted feasibility study should give a reasonably good indication of the likelihood of major gift support from an institution's top-level benefactors. The sample of interviewees must be sufficient to allow those conducting the study to draw conclusions about the likelihood of major support. An accurate and timely feasibility study is the only way to determine the size of the capital campaign goal.

Need Goal Versus Dollar Goal

Institutions should not back away from communicating—both to internal and external constituents—progress in relation to dollar goals—assuming those dollar goals are a reasonable expression of what the institution can raise in a relatively short period. The public is interested in tracking the progress toward the dollar goal, and institutions have an obligation to report it. But it is also wise to consider communicating progress toward the specific needs and priorities the institution has identified as campaign priorities. Campaigns are not ends in themselves, but means to an end—to strengthen the institution for more effective service to its constituencies by shoring up programs, facilities, equipment, and, above all, educational quality. Thus, colleges and universities need to go beyond generalities and discuss the specifics of their campaigns. How well is the institution progressing on raising funds for scholarships, for endowed faculty positions, for facilities and equipment, and for other endowed programs? Which academic and administrative units within the institution are meeting or exceeding their "needs" and which are not?

It is vitally important for all institutional constituencies—faculty, students, staff, alumni, governing boards, legislators, and the general public—to know that the institution is raising funds for specific needs. Thus, progress should be reported in terms of the institutional needs statement as well as the overall dollar goal. As will be seen in chapter 8, the new campaign reporting standards of CASE specifically recommend this documentation in periodic campaign reports.

Excesses will put institutions at risk not only with external constituencies but with faculty and students as well. When faculty and students see institutions announcing that they have raised more than $100 million in a capital campaign, yet only $10 million of that total is actually in the bank, institutions can expect skepticism and mistrust.

Philanthropic Giving to Public Universities

One of the most difficult tasks facing a public university engaged in a major private gifts campaign is to convincingly respond to a question often asked by potential donors: "Why should I make private gifts to an institution that is supposedly sustained by state or municipal tax revenues?"

The line between independent and public colleges and universities has always been blurred at best. The earliest American institutions of higher education were generally religious enterprises, yet they invariably received some form of government assistance. Today, federal and state governments allocate billions of dollars annually to independent institutions in the form of research contracts, fellowships and scholarships, guaranteed student loans, and other benefits.[12]

Public colleges and universities bear tremendous responsibilities for undergraduate education and research. Public higher education institutions enroll nearly 80 percent of the nation's approximately 12 million undergraduates.[13] These students can go on to become some of the nation's most productive and influential citizens.

Public institutions produce the overwhelming majority of the nation's engineers. More than half the presidents and board chairpersons of the Fortune 500 companies are alumni of public institutions.[14] Public institutions receive about half of all funds allocated for research in American universities. The land-grant institutions, especially, have excelled in agricultural research. Public universities make up half the membership in the prestigious Association of American Universities, a consortium of 56 outstanding research institutions.

Higher education is the engine in an information-driven society. The federal government has recognized this through its land-grant legislation and continues to offer strong support. But it is also up to the private sector to make certain that the engine of higher education performs up to its capacity. State support of public universities continues to dwindle throughout the nation, and many publicly funded institutions now claim to be publicly assisted. Support from the state tax dollar has fallen below 40 percent, and, in some institutions, below 30 percent of total revenues. Private support is absolutely vital to the public university and will become increasingly more important as tax support continues to decline.

Selecting a Campaign Name or Theme

Many institutions spend an inordinate amount of time determining a campaign name or theme. Some years ago, *CASE CURRENTS* magazine printed a handy model for determining the name of a capital campaign.[15] This model has recently been updated, and both are included in appendix D.

While the name of a campaign may be important to certain constituencies, it does not have a material impact on the success of the effort. The simpler the name of the campaign the better, and the use of catch phrases and overused expressions (i.e., "The Campaign for Excellence") should be avoided. A simplistic but effective formulation is: "The Campaign for (Institution's Name)."

Notes

1. Robert L. Krit, *The Fund-Raising Handbook.* (The United States of America: Scott Foresman Professional Books, 1991), p. 13.
2. Kent E. Dove, *Conducting a Successful Capital Campaign: A Comprehensive Guide for Nonprofit Organizations.* (San Francisco: Jossey-Bass Inc., 1988), p. 7.
3. H. Russell Bintzer, "The Many Uses of Professional Counsel," in Francis C. Pray, ed., *Handbook for Educational Fund Raising: A Guide to Successful Principles and Practices for Colleges, Universities and Schools* (San Francisco: Jossey-Bass Inc., 1981), p. 217.
4. Jerold Panas, *How to Choose the Right Fund Raising Firm.* (Chicago: Young & Partners, Inc.). [Pamphlet]
5. Bintzer, "The Many Uses of Professional Counsel," in *Handbook for Educational Fund Raising: A Guide to Successful Principles and Practices for Colleges, Universities and Schools,* p. 218.
6. Krit, *The Fund-Raising Handbook,* p. 17.
7. Kent E. Dove, "Changing Strategies for Meeting Campaign Goals," in A. Westley Rowland, ed., *Handbook of Institutional Advancement: A Modern Guide to Executive Management, Institutional Relations, Fund-Raising, Alumni Administration, Government Relations, Publications, Periodicals, and Enrollment Management* (San Francisco: Jossey-Bass Inc., 1986) pp. 292–309.
8. Richard Page Allen, "Testing the Market: The Feasibility Study," in H. Gerald Quigg, ed., *The Successful Capital Campaign: From Planning to Victory Celebration* (Washington, D.C.: Council for the Advancement and Support of Education, 1986), p. 31.
9. John J. Schwartz, "Role and Selection of Professional Counsel," in A. Westley Rowland, ed., *Handbook of Institutional Advancement: A Modern Guide to Executive Management, Institutional Relations, Fund-Raising, Alumni Administration, Government Relations, Publications, Periodicals, and Enrollment Management* 2nd ed. (San Francisco: Jossey-Bass Inc., 1986), pp. 351–354.
10. Allen, "Testing the Market: The Feasibility Study," in *The Successful Capital Campaign: From Planning to Victory Celebration,* pp. 31–35.
11. Robert L. Stuhr, "The Case Statement," in James L. Fisher and G. H. Quehl, *The President and Fund Raising.* (New York: American Council on Education and Macmillan Publishing Company, 1989), pp. 55–62.

12. The Chronicle of Higher Education, *The Chronicle of Higher Education Almanac vol. xxxix no. 1:* (August 26, 1992): 34.
13. The Chronicle of Higher Education, *The Chronicle of Higher Education Almanac vol. xxxix no. 1:* (August 26, 1992): 11.
14. Robert L. Clodius, "The Essential Partnership," in *Serving the World: The People and the Ideas of America's State and Land-Grant Universities.* (Washington, DC: National Association of State Universities and Land-Grant Colleges, 1987).
15. Bernice A. Thieblot, "Name that Campaign," *CASE CURRENTS vol. v no. 3:* (March, 1979): 58 and *vol. xx no. 10:* (November/ December, 1994): 58.

THREE

Creating a Campaign Organization

The decision has been made to move forward vigorously on a capital campaign. The president is supportive, the governing board has given its approval, the feasibility study indicates that resources are available among alumni and other constituents, and the academic leadership of the institution has prioritized those needs most critical for funding by the campaign. Now it becomes imperative to create a campaign organization that will get the job done.

This is no small task. Creating a campaign organization cannot wait until all of the elements mentioned in chapters 1 and 2 are in place. Instead, the process must move forward simultaneously with those elements. The campaign organization must be in place, or at least substantially in place, before the feasibility study is complete. Even if the study suggests objectives to reach before a campaign begins, staff can work on reaching these goals.

Integration of Institutional Advancement— The First Step

Capital campaigns are managed by professional support staff under the direction of the chief development officer. The notion of combining fund raising with the other two traditional external-relation positions—university or college relations and alumni relations—under the authority of a single officer was first proposed at the so-called Greenbriar Conference of 1958, where a number of higher education public relations personnel met to discuss institutional advancement.[1] Since then, virtually all professionals and research scholars working in the field have endorsed this concept. However, until recently, little attention has been paid to whether it makes a difference if a development, university relations, and alumni relations program is organized on an integrated (i.e., centralized under one office) or nonintegrated (noncentralized) basis *when preparing* for a capital campaign.

A survey of senior advancement officers at 10 major research universities nationwide, who at that time were engaged in capital campaigns, helped to answer this question.[2] Five of the universities used integrated organizations in planning and initiating their campaigns. At these institutions, the top four officers—the head of each of the three components and the vice president to whom they reported—were interviewed. The other five institutions used nonintegrated organization structures. Here only the three component heads were queried, because a vice president over the entire institutional advancement component did not exist.

A capital campaign is an intense, time-consuming project of formidable complexity. The study concluded that universities that have integrated organizational structures will be better able to prepare for their campaigns, achieving cost savings and better utilization of existing staff. Unhealthy competition among advancement units also is likely to be reduced.[3]

It is only logical, then, to recommend that the integrated organization be implemented *before* the campaign is initiated. The preparation of the case statement, the creation and continued monitoring of public relations plans, the production of campaign videos and publications, and the impaneling of volunteers can be enhanced through integration.

The critical first step in creating a campaign organization, therefore, is to create a vice president-level position that has authority over all institutional advancement, including university or college relations, alumni relations, and development.

The person occupying this senior role should be an individual with a development background and solid fund-raising expertise. This is not to denigrate the other components of the advancement function. It is simply a recognition of the fact that the institutional advancement component of a university must move in unison during a capital campaign, and all three units must come together to support, enhance, and promote campaign objectives. Without this cooperation, the campaign will not move forward as rapidly or as efficiently as the president and the governing board would like. Capital campaign success requires teamwork, and this teamwork can only be accomplished by integrating and centralizing the advancement function. An organizational chart for the advancement function at a college or university may be found in appendix E.

Internal Planning Group

The first step in staffing a campaign is to form an internal planning group consisting of those individuals who will provide the ongoing support to the effort. This group should be chaired by the chief advancement officer. Its purpose is to lay out the basic components and the timetable of the campaign and to track the efforts involved. Initially, the planning group should meet on a weekly basis and continue to meet throughout the campaign, never less frequently than once a month.

All major decision making should flow from this internal committee. Recommendations to the president, to the campaign chairperson, and to other volunteer leaders should begin with this committee. This internal planning group should provide the agenda for volunteer-committee meetings, decisions on solicitations, the lead brochure, and supporting audio-visual materials. Obviously, not every decision can be made by the internal committee, as some decisions will need to go before the president, the governing board, or the volunteers. However, the discussion that will form the basis for decision making should take place in this committee. The internal committee is the nerve center of the entire campaign and can even be referred to as the campaign cabinet, which guides, directs, and supports *all* campaign initiatives.

In addition to the chief development or institutional advancement officer, members of this internal committee should include:

- **Development Officer in Charge of Prospect Management.** This could be the director of development, assistant director of development, or major gifts officer in charge of tracking major gifts solicitation for the institution. In small institutions this individual might very well wear several hats. Whoever is working primarily with major gift prospects should be a member of this internal group.

- **Constituent Relations or Donor Relations Officer.** The person in charge of donor relations for the institution should be a member of the group, because the planning of events, provision of donor premiums, and fulfillment of donor expectations will become very important in the early stages of the campaign.
- **Director of College or University Relations, Public Relations, or Public Information.** In an integrated system where this officer reports to a vice president for advancement, he or she should be put on the internal planning group. A number of initiatives involving development communications—including press releases, video presentations, brochures, and press conferences—will require the expertise of a public relations professional. Integrating this important function into the campaign is vital in the early stages of the effort.
- **Publications Director.** Many times in an integrated system, the publications officer reports to the director of university relations. If this is not the case, then this official should be a member of the internal group. The planning of internal and external publications can take many months, and including the publications director early on in the project will facilitate the preparation of these materials.
- Other personnel who should be members of the internal planning group depend upon the organization and structure of the institution involved. Suffice it to say that this group should be composed of all of those persons who can help to move the campaign forward because of the scope of their responsibility at the institution.

Staffing Required

The number of staff members required for a capital campaign will, of course, depend upon the scope and size of the institution. Certain positions are necessary, however, for a campaign of any size. Speaking in approximations, in large public research universities the staff could range from 75 to 150 people, and perhaps beyond. At institutions with enrollments of 1,000 to 3,000 people, staff size is most likely to range between 5 and 25 people.

■ **The Campaign Director.** The campaign director is the senior official leading and guiding the campaign on a day-to-day basis. He or she must give the campaign total and complete attention. The campaign is the director's life. He or she thinks about the campaign first thing in the morning and the last thing at the end of the day. It is a job that requires complete and total attention to campaign goals and objectives and should not be undermined by less important priorities.

The chief development officer or vice president of the advancement program should become the director of the campaign. After all, by this juncture the president of the college or university and the governing board have determined that the campaign will be the most important program launched at the institution over the next four-to-six years. Pivotal campaign decisions will need to be made by the vice president, and establishing a layer below the vice president can create an unnecessary bureaucratic organizational structure.

This does not mean, however, that the vice president should necessarily take on the title of director of the campaign. Many large, highly successful campaigns do not have a staff position titled director of the campaign, preferring that this task be performed by the vice president in charge of institutional advancement or development. Senior administrators, the governing board, and volunteers need to agree that the person directing the campaign on a daily basis should be the highest officer of the advancement division. That signal sends a strong message about the critical nature of the campaign.[4]

If the vice president does take on the responsibilities of director of the campaign, then it is necessary to employ additional personnel in the vice president's office to assist with the ongoing, noncampaign programs. An administrative assistant, development assistant, or development officer can help immeasurably in this regard.

Many relatively inexperienced development professionals in senior positions ask, "How can I do the work I am doing now and be campaign director all at the same time?" The answer, of course, is that when the decision has been made to move forward on the planning of the capital campaign, practically *everything* the vice president does should be related in some way to the capital campaign. The vice president must reprogram and reevaluate duties and responsibilities that do not directly influence campaign activity. The vice president's entire agenda should be focused on getting the capital campaign up and running. To focus on items that are not related to the campaign is to do an injustice to the institution.

- **The Director of Prospect Management.** How many individuals are assigned to prospect management depends on the size and scope of the institution. Some institutions—those with several hundred thousand alumni—have prospect management staffs of half a dozen people who are constantly reviewing and updating prospect lists. However, every campaign needs at least one professional to develop the major gift solicitation list. In most cases it is a full-time job requiring comprehensive knowledge of the institution, its alumni and friends, and major benefactors.

- **Director of Research.** Many smaller institutions ignore the research function at this stage. Research seems to be the last office filled in many development operations. Nevertheless, it is a vital component of a capital campaign and cannot be overlooked as staff is organized in contemplation of a capital effort. Penn State employed as many as eight full-time research coordinators during the initial stages of its first capital campaign. Even an institution with fewer than 1,000 students would be advised to employ at least one individual on the development staff with research skills.

  The research staff should identify potential major gift prospects. It is a process that should begin long before the capital campaign is launched. The staff member in charge of research should develop profiles on individual, corporate, and foundation prospects having the potential to make gifts of $25,000 and above. A general rule of thumb requires 10 prospects to ensure one major gift to the capital campaign. A 10 percent success rate may, in fact, be high without a strong history of major gifts. Individual profiles of major gift prospects should be completed long before the feasibility study is ever undertaken.

- **Director of Corporate and Foundation Relations.** This position is essential at a large research university, but a staff member ideally should be assigned to this area of the campaign even at smaller institutions.

As a rule, corporations and foundations do not make unrestricted gifts or support endowments or bricks-and-mortar projects. There will generally be a need for a *quid pro quo* for a corporate donor to make a major campaign commitment to any institution, public or independent, large or small. Corporations have become notorious for requiring some tangible benefit in return for their "generosity."

These benefits can range from special student recruitment privileges to sponsorship of academic research programs. At a major research university, these "project-oriented proposals" can be extraordinarily time consuming and will require the diligence of dedicated staff members, who will work with faculty in applied research areas to develop proposals that match the interests and opportunities of a particular corporate entity. An automobile manufacturer might be interested in the mechanical engineering curriculum, while major oil companies might be most supportive of programs to enhance oil recovery. Major support from the corporate sector is more readily available to the research university than the small, independent liberal arts institution. However, this is not to say that small colleges do not have opportunities for major corporate gifts, especially if these institutions are located near corporate centers or key branches.

- **Director of Annual Giving.** Annual giving at a college or university must continue, even during the capital campaign years. There must be a staff member who sufficiently understands the relationship between the campaign and annual giving to keep the annual giving component of the institution alive and well. In a small shop, this person has additional responsibilities. At a large university, the director of annual giving may have a rather large staff used to interfacing with colleges, development officers, and deans. In any case, annual giving must be protected from atrophying during the campaign years.
- **Director of Donor or Constituent Relations.** Increased philanthropic support to a college or university presents unprecedented opportunities for the strengthening of donor relations. Benefactors who make major commitments to an institution require special care and attention. Someone who makes a $100,000 commitment will expect—and deserve—instant response to inquiries about a whole variety of institutional matters.

A staff member should be assigned to the care and well-being of these benefactors, not only during the life of the campaign but afterwards as well. Major gift activity increases the intensity of this office dramatically, so this staff member should also be physically located close to the chief development officer or vice president. Major gift prospects and donors tend to want to deal with the chief officer of the development program. Situating the head of donor relations/constituent relations in the vice president's office will give benefactors the sense that they are dealing with the top institutional advancement officer and are not being shunted to a lesser staff member who has correspondingly less "clout" within the institution.

- **Proposal Writer.** Every campaign, regardless of size, needs at least one proposal writer. This writer will not only be in charge of corporate and foundation proposal writing, a process that is often technical and faculty driven, but also will fashion proposals for individual contributors. *Every individual solicited for a major campaign gift should receive a formal, specifically tailored proposal.* As will be discussed later, casual solicitations—by phone, mail, or in person—that do not use a written proposal can be disastrous. Preparing these proposals is essential to the success of any capital campaign. A staff member who can help produce the proposals in a timely, efficient, and diligent manner is crucial.

- **Director of Development Communications.** All campaigns, large or small, produce communications with internal and external audiences. A staff member must possess excellent written and verbal skills to effectively produce campaign brochures, newsletters, press releases, and overall news media relations. In an integrated university, this individual could be the chief public relations or university relations officer. In the small shop, this individual will likely have numerous responsibilities. In any event, there needs to be at least one staff member who understands this component of the capital campaign and can provide support and assistance in shaping campaign communications.

- **Development Officers Overseeing Fund-Raising Personnel.** An active volunteer campaign committee requires close supervision and support by the development staff. For example, trained, knowledgeable development officers should accompany volunteers on fund-raising calls. These officers should not be burdened with heavy managerial responsibility or the day-to-day operations of the campaign. They must be readily accessible and able to travel the majority of the time, and they must respond quickly and efficiently to volunteers during intense proposal delivery activity. At a large research institution with multiple campuses, there may be as many as 20 or 30 individuals assigned this responsibility, including the vice president, who accompanies senior administrators and volunteers when calling on prospects at the highest level. In a small shop, the vice president and two or three staff members with multiple responsibilities might serve this function. Persons assigned this responsibility should be among the most talented and experienced development staff members. These are the people on the front lines, cultivating potential donors and "selling" the campaign to institutional constituents.

Although it is difficult for the vice president of development to find time for this activity, it is essential that he or she be seen as the chief fund raiser (after the president). The vice president must, therefore, reserve considerable time for direct, face-to-face solicitation.

- **Director of Records Systems.** Major gift donors will expect their commitments to be tracked, recorded, and acknowledged efficiently and effectively. A staff member who carries out this function is critical to the success of the capital campaign. Gift commitments must be recorded by an institution with extreme care and extraordinary accuracy. Failure to record a gift or to properly acknowledge the gift can have a deleterious effect on future major gift support.

- **Director of Planned Giving.** Whether the capital campaign is being conducted at a large research university or a small, independent liberal arts college, a highly competent deferred-giving officer is essential. In the large institution environment, several planned gift officers may be necessary (in 1994, Penn State had four planned gift officers). In a small environment, the vice president or director of development may be called upon to fill this role. Whichever the case, irrevocable deferred/planned gifts may account for well over 50 percent of the goal of a capital campaign. Knowledgeable personnel, trained in the latest gift techniques, will be important.

Each of the staff positions described above is instrumental for the successful launching and efficient running of a capital campaign and should not be overlooked due to lack of resources. At a major institution each of these components might be staffed by several individuals. At a small college, one individual might be charged with administering two or more of the components.

Experience has shown that a capital campaign invariably requires many more staff members than assumed at the outset. Presidents and governing boards are usually surprised and sometimes even dismayed at the number of new personnel required to make the campaign a success. It is simply not possible to run a capital campaign with existing development and university/college relations personnel, and increased personnel costs are a fact of life. If the president of an institution requires the chief development officer to administer the campaign without any increased staff, that president is dooming the effort to failure and is asking the chief development officer to accomplish the impossible. The capital campaign *will require* increased personnel costs in practically every sector of the development operation.[5]

Relationship of the Capital Campaign to Ongoing Fund-Raising Activities

A sophisticated development organization is in the business of raising money, with or without the aegis of a capital campaign. This has even led to the argument among some development professionals that capital campaigns are simply an ongoing statement of institutional needs and priorities and that institutions should continue to vigorously raise private funds with or without the framework of a capital campaign. After all, just because the campaign has concluded does not mean that the needs of an institution cease to be acute. In fact, a capital campaign tends to raise the level of expectation among academic administrators for continued resources for academic priorities.

Some development professionals agree that an institution is always in a capital campaign because that institution is *always* seeking private gift support as vigorously as possible. The University of Texas—Austin has long felt that the formal establishment of a capital campaign is not necessary because it continually seeks private gift support year in and year out. In other words, the institution's entire program is trying to seek the maximum support possible from alumni, friends, corporations, and foundations. Therefore, the trappings of a capital campaign are superfluous.

In a sense, what the officials at the University of Texas—Austin are saying is that the capital campaign simply "gets in the way" of ongoing fund-raising activities. Their argument rebuffs the proposition that it is impossible to sustain an intensified, systematic program of major gift fund raising on an ongoing basis, that there is no opportunity to "rally the troops" around a particular cause, and that volunteers grow weary of major gift fund raising after five to seven years. The University of Texas contends that it *is* possible to sustain major gift fund raising forever. Unfortunately, a sustained, intense major gift fund-raising campaign or activity will many times lead to "donor fatigue." Benefactors will, in fact, grow weary of perpetual major gift solicitation without some relief.

There is no question that a five- to seven-year capital campaign instills a fund-raising process that will continue to benefit the institution in years ahead. While the day-to-day development activities should by no means be suspended during a campaign, all components of a development operation should be keyed into campaign activities. None of the ongoing activities should exist in a vacuum apart from the overall campaign activity; each should run in tandem with the campaign.

Annual Fund

Regardless of the size of the institution, the vast majority of a college or university's alumni will not be given the benefit of a personal call by a volunteer or staff member on behalf of the campaign. It is simply not feasible or practical for vast numbers of alumni to be contacted personally and asked to make a gift to the campaign. At Penn State, the database lists 350,000 alumni. A personalized appeal to only 1 percent of these would require 3,500 personal solicitations. Similarly, at a small college with 10,000 to 20,000 alumni, the proportionally smaller professional staff size still makes it difficult to call on a large percentage of this database population.

Nevertheless, an annual fund program should not continue during the campaign without regard for the larger effort. Many institutions have left the annual giving program undisturbed during the capital campaign and have focused on major gifts from a relatively small number of alumni. Under this scenario, annual giving is allowed to send the same type of mailings and perform the same kind of telephone solicitations that it has always done. Communications with alumni proceed as if the capital campaign does not exist.

This is a mistake. The annual fund program should continue to seek gifts during the capital campaign, but should recognize the campaign in all promotional literature. A 1979 survey of universities conducting capital campaigns by the American Council on Education found that "in both the public and private sectors, the overwhelming majority of institutions maintain their annual fund-raising programs during the course of their capital campaigns."[6]

Annual fund literature should carry a description of the campaign, and alumni should be made to feel that their annual gifts are helping, even in a small way, to satisfy campaign needs. Extreme care, however, should be taken to make certain that alumni do not feel their annual gift is necessarily their *only* gift to the capital campaign. Many alumni who are solicited for an annual gift of $100, $500, or $1,000 might inadvertently be made to feel that they have done all that is necessary for the capital campaign. If so, a future solicitation of a particular alumnus for a gift of $25,000, $50,000, or $100,000 might fall on deaf ears. An alumnus should not feel that his or her annual gift relieves him or her of an obligation to make a major gift to the campaign.

This is likely to be a problem with only that small percentage of alumni who are capable of making a major gift to the campaign. There are several ways to avoid what can be called a *preemptive annual gift* (see figure 3.1).

Corporate and Foundation Relations

In many cases, capital campaigns present an opportunity to increase annual gift or normal ongoing support from a corporation or a foundation to the institution. If the college or university is receiving $10,000 a year for a particular project from XYZ Corporation, it might be possible to invite that corporation to pledge that amount during the life of the campaign as well as increase it to new levels. In this case, the use of a double-ask, where the campaign solicitation includes an annual giving component, can work

Figure 3.1 Ways of Avoiding a Preemptive Annual Gift

The following actions can help institutions avoid a preemptive annual gift:

1. Delete from annual phone or mail gift solicitation databases those major gift prospects who will be asked personally to contribute to the campaign with a multiple-year pledge. Even though this mechanism solves the problem of receiving a preemptive gift through the mail, it is not recommended under all circumstances. Unless the capital campaign has a large staff that is capable of reaching alumni quickly, it could mean that certain alumni will go unsolicited for several months, if not for several years, during the campaign. Excluding an alumnus from an annual fund mailing solicitation in an attempt to reserve him or her for a capital campaign "ask" may simply have the effect of "losing the annual gift." Extreme caution should be taken when making any decision to eliminate major gift prospects from the annual giving process.

2. Isolate major gift prospects and deal with them through special mailings that inform and educate the prospects to the necessity of a "double ask." The double ask appeals to an alumnus or friend of the institution to make a commitment, not only to annual giving, but a multiyear pledge to the capital campaign as well. The double ask does require the education of alumni and must be carefully worded so that alumni keep the commitments separate and distinct.

3. A third option is to continue annual giving appeals full throttle, and, in fact, make them a part of the overall campaign by using the campaign logo and campaign information in all annual fund literature. Major gift prospects receive the same mailings as all other prospects, and these mailings are identified as campaign-related solicitations. When the alumni are called upon personally and individually by staff and volunteers for major gifts, an explanation is made for the necessity of both annual giving and capital giving. The second solicitation (the campaign solicitation) is structured and likened to other philanthropic giving, most particularly, church giving. Most religious organizations ask for ongoing annual giving for church or synagogue operations. Occasionally, members of a particular church or synagogue are asked to contribute a capital gift for a particular project that has been identified as a priority. Generally, this is a bricks-and-mortar project, but not necessarily. Most individuals recognize the difference between an annual gift and a capital gift with a multiyear pledge.

Figure 3.1 (Continued)

4. Finally, it might be wise to consider suspending phone and mail solicitation to major prospects during the life of the campaign. Many smaller institutions have chosen this alternative and have asked these prospects to make a multiyear commitment to annual giving as well as a multiyear commitment to the capital campaign. In other words, ask an alumnus to continue his or her $1,000 annual gift, and pledge an additional capital gift over the next five years to a scholarship fund or other endowed fund or project. Remind the alumnus of both his annual and capital gift at the same time. Hendrix College used this strategy very effectively in a campaign in the early 1980s. Major gift alumni are asked for one commitment with two components. Again, however, the problem of getting to all of these major gift prospects in a relatively short period of time is a drawback to this process.

---

especially well. When asking a corporation for a campaign gift, do not simply ignore the annual component that is already coming from the corporation. Make it a part of the overall solicitation.

For many years, corporations and foundations resisted appeals for capital campaigns. These entities did not generally give to bricks-and-mortar projects and endowment funds anyway, and they appeared disinterested in learning about campaign priorities. There is some evidence that this is changing, and corporate executives are beginning to understand the importance of a capital campaign to an institution. Jon Van Til and Associates state that "increasingly, corporate giving is being seen not solely as philanthropy but rather as an established part of doing business."[7]

Planned Giving

The planned giving office is a key component of a capital campaign team. Many of the larger commitments during any campaign are in the form of planned, irrevocable gifts that require the expertise and knowledge of a professional planned gift office. Pressure will build to accelerate planned gifts so that they are in a form that allows for their countability in the campaign. Planned gift staff should always exercise flexibility in looking for ways to move gifts to fruition while maintaining the integrity of the major gift process. This sense of urgency is the major difference between a planned giving staff in a campaign mode and one in a noncampaign environment. Pressure to accept major planned gifts, irrevocable in nature, as opposed to smaller cash gifts will also be in evidence. Staff must balance these competing needs, always focusing on what is best for the institution as a whole.

Communications

All communications with the institution's constituencies during the life of the campaign should reflect the status of a campaign environment. Internal and external publications should clearly be identified as campaign publications. If an institution has previously done a good job of communicating to its constituencies, there is no reason to change the general format, and only minor adjustments need to be made to signal that these existing publications are campaign-oriented. Perhaps a name change of a particular communications deliverable is all that would be necessary. However, all communication techniques should be seen as campaign communication pieces during the lifetime of the effort.

The Volunteer Organization

The campaign gives the institution the opportunity to revitalize and reinvigorate its main volunteer organization. Many colleges and universities have a major volunteer organization composed of alumni and friends who assist in the development function. These organizations should not necessarily be suspended during the campaign. However, because the capital campaign does allow an institution to redirect the focus of the major volunteer group, in some cases an existing volunteer group should be put "on hold" so that a new volunteer organization can be created exclusively to support the campaign.

At Penn State, for example, a development council existed in 1984, when the university was preparing for a capital campaign. The council was composed primarily of individuals who, while supportive of the university, did not have the financial capability to make major commitments. Moreover, the council was suffering from burnout. Penn State decided to place this organization on hold and created a new organization titled The Executive Committee of the Campaign. When the campaign concluded six years later, a new organization was formed with *new members* and renamed The National Development Council. The new membership did include many of the volunteers who were active during The Campaign for Penn State. Only the volunteers that exhibited interest in garnering financial resources for the institution were invited back on the council. This afforded nonactive members the opportunity to quietly serve the university in other ways.

Thus a whole new organization sprang from the campaign volunteer group. The National Development Council has proven to be more vigorous and supportive of university projects than its precampaign predecessor, and it is composed of individuals who have the financial ability and wherewithal to make major commitments to the university.

Do not allow two volunteer organizations to operate simultaneously during the campaign. It is not possible for staff members to service both groups, and confusion will exist as to the purposes and functions of one volunteer group versus the other, unhealthy competitor.

At those public universities with foundations composed of volunteers who control the fund-raising programs of the institution, the campaign volunteer committee should come from that organization or at least be made a subunit of that organization. The preferred technique is to use the existing foundation board of directors as the campaign committee. This may not be possible if the board is not composed of major gift prospects who can guide, lead, and direct the campaign through the example of their own philanthropy.

The Role of the President of the Institution in the Campaign

The president has a dramatic impact on the campaign. As stated previously, the president must totally support the concept of a campaign and must be its strongest advocate. He or she must make the campaign an institutional priority and devote a substantial percentage of time to the effort. In their book, *The President and Fund Raising*, James Fisher and G.H. Quehl state that "the college or university president must lead the entire fund-raising effort as the chief advancement officer for the institution."[8]

How much of the president's time should the campaign require? In the early stages of the effort, it is not out of the realm of possibility for a president to devote as much as 60 to 70 percent of his or her time to campaign priorities. At a minimum, the president must be willing to devote ample time to the following activities.

Assisting with and Endorsing the Campaign Planning Phase

The president must be viewed as the campaign leader. This cannot be left to the campaign staff or the chief development officer. As the person who will bring the campaign to fruition, he or she must be at the front of any planning efforts.

Recruiting the Volunteer Committee for the Campaign

The president must be willing to travel extensively in the early days of the effort to impanel the volunteer committee for the campaign. Again, this cannot be left to the chief development officer. The president must personally recruit every member of the main volunteer committee. Recruitment should include personal calls, either at the volunteer's home or place of business. Securing the campaign chairperson will probably be the most important initial task of the president.

Attending Meetings of the Volunteer Group

The president must attend every meeting of the major volunteer group of the campaign to demonstrate to these volunteers that the campaign is an important priority. Major volunteers will want to communicate directly with the president about campaign matters, and he or she should be available accordingly.

Acting as Principal Spokesperson for the Campaign

All major gift announcements should flow through the president's office and be made jointly by the president and the campaign chairperson. This demonstrates to benefactors that their gift commitments are considered vital and will also signal internal and external constituencies that the campaign is very important to the welfare of the institution.

Participating in the Faculty/Staff Campaign

The president should be a visible and active participant during the internal faculty/staff campaign. The president must be seen as totally supportive of the effort, and this visibility will serve as a multiplier, encouraging other members of the faculty/staff community to make commitments to the campaign.

Soliciting Major Gifts

Generally speaking, the president should solicit any gift above $250,000; donors will expect it. Corporate and foundation gifts in the $1 million range should be solicited by the president. Obviously, the president will have a very high profile in campaigns of $100 million or more because these larger-scale efforts require numerous gifts of $250,000 and above. Presidential involvement below the $250,000 level should be evaluated closely. This is particularly true in larger institutions. Smaller colleges and universities might appropriately reduce this level to perhaps $100,000 but much below this becomes a poor use of the president's time. The CEO of the institution must concentrate on major, sizable gifts. Only in circumstances where the president has a close personal relationship with the prospect should his or her involvement be considered below this level. Certainly, the president of the university should solicit the chairperson of the campaign early on regardless of the size of the chairperson's campaign commitment.

Role of the Chief Institutional Advancement Officer—(Vice President)

In any major gift campaign, the chief advancement officer, usually at the vice presidential level, inevitably has a very high profile. Duties and responsibilities follow.

Providing Staff Support to the Chairperson and President

First and foremost, the vice president must provide staff support to the chairperson of the campaign and the president of the institution. All prospects assigned to the chairperson of the campaign and the president must also be assigned to the vice president. The vice president should know these prospects intimately and view them as his or hers under the prospect management system.

Any time a solicitation is made by the chairperson or president, the vice president should promptly debrief the chairperson and the president. The vice president should provide written reports of contact, even though he or she may not actually make the solicitation with the president or chairperson. In short, the vice president provides support to the president and campaign chairperson on an ongoing basis and makes certain that reports of contact, proposal letters, and acknowledgment letters are done in a timely and efficient manner.

Supporting the chairperson and the president is the most critical and important priority of the vice president. In any major gift campaign, the chairperson and the president should be involved on a weekly basis in gift solicitations. Servicing these two important officials will occupy a great deal of time by the vice president, but no task is more important during the campaign's major gift solicitation phase.

Serving as Liaison to the Volunteer Committee

The vice president also is the staff liaison to the top volunteer committee. The vice president's office should maintain constant contact with the top volunteer committee. The vice president must remain in monthly contact with all members of the volunteer committee, either through phone conversations or personal visitations. Members of the volunteer committee should feel comfortable with the vice president on a personal basis and should be willing to contact the vice president at any time with important campaign information, particularly regarding new prospects.

Serving as Campaign Director

As already noted, the vice president should serve as the director of the campaign. This responsibility should not be delegated to any other official. Major volunteers and benefactors of the institution will want to deal not only with the president but with the senior fund-raising official. The vice president must plan and direct the campaign on a daily basis, and provide analysis of every aspect of campaign activity, plans, and fund-raising potential. Many administrative details of the campaign can be assigned to other staff members, but responsibility for moving the campaign forward on a day-to-day basis should remain with the vice president.

Providing Services to the Campaign Committee Meetings

All meetings of campaign committees should be under the direction of the chief development officer. The agenda and major thrusts of campaign meetings should flow from the vice president, in consultation with campaign volunteers.

Soliciting Major Gifts

The vice president can and should accompany the president of the university and/or the chairperson of the campaign on major gift solicitations. Care should be taken that no more than three individuals be involved in a solicitation at any one time. Generally speaking, the vice president makes a $1 million solicitation only if accompanied by a campaign volunteer or the president of the institution. The vice president is involved in solicitations at the level of $100,000 to $1 million. Obviously, there are exceptions to this general rule and the solicitations will depend upon the vice president's relationship with campaign prospects. The vice president is one of the major solicitors during the campaign and should be expected to spend 50 percent to 75 percent of his or her time in campaign solicitations during the advanced gift phase of the campaign. Given the administrative tasks that the vice president will be required to perform, this will be very difficult to accomplish. The vice president will be the busiest individual in the campaign and must protect his or her time carefully.

No major campaign meeting should take place without the involvement of the vice president, nor should any major solicitation move forward without his or her knowledge and approval. All agendas of campaign committee meetings should be structured and approved by the vice president. In short, the vice president is the director, the architect, the progenitor, the manager, and the facilitator for the entire campaign. Without a strong vice president guiding and leading the effort, the campaign cannot be successful. The president and lead volunteers must have a vice president who is hardworking, diligent, energetic, and enthusiastic, and who is always looking for the next major gift to the campaign. During the intense period of the campaign, the vice president should think about the campaign 18 hours a day. The other six hours are reserved for sleep and reflection.

Throughout this chapter, the chief advancement officer has

been referred to as a vice president-level official of the college or university. It is strongly urged that the person occupying this position hold that title. The institution relies on this person to guide and lead a critically important university priority, and the title of vice president is an outward sign to constituents of the importance of the position.

Role of the Director of Alumni Relations

In any capital campaign, the director of alumni relations must be an enthusiastic supporter of the effort, as many alumni traditionally look to this official first for guidance and direction.

The alumni magazine should regularly carry stories and articles about campaign successes. In fact, the alumni director should make space in alumni publications available to the campaign office on a continuing basis. The director and staff should also make campaign news a priority during alumni club visitations. They should make presentations on the importance of the campaign at all public alumni meetings and should be willing to share campaign materials and information readily with alumni throughout the country.

It is not out of the realm of possibility to involve the director of alumni directly in campaign solicitations. Many times, alumni directors are closer to alumni prospects than any other individual at the institution. Involving them in the solicitation phase, provided they have expertise in solicitation, can yield important benefits. Even though an alumni director's main responsibility is generally "friend raising," there is no reason why this cannot be expanded to fund raising during the life of the campaign.

Furthermore, in many campaigns, alumni clubs have been encouraged to create endowed scholarships and fellowships. Depending upon campaign priorities, it may be advisable to encourage alumni clubs to be involved in the campaign at this level.

Many alumni associations have independent funds available for the use of their board of directors. It would not be unusual, then, to ask the directors to appropriate funds to the campaign as a gift from the association. At Penn State the Alumni Association made a $1 million gift to endowment programs. This gift was collected mainly from self-generated revenue, including the sale of alumni watches, clothing, credit cards, and licensing fees. The gift had a dramatic impact on alumni giving in general and served as a multiplier, inspiring contributions from other independent university groups.

If support from the alumni director is important to the campaign, it is only reasonable to conclude that criticism about campaign priorities and a less than supportive attitude on behalf of the alumni director can undermine campaign priorities. Consequently, it is imperative that the alumni director be kept informed, involved, and a part of the campaign at every juncture.

Role of the College or University Relations Director

Titles for this individual vary from institution to institution, but the responsibilities are mainly those of a chief public relations officer, who is in charge of public relations, public information, and media relations. For the purposes of this book, this person is referred to as director of college or university relations.

In an integrated program where this official reports to the chief advancement officer, the director of university relations should be intimately involved in the campaign. When a separate development communications program is not in effect, the director of university relations along with his or her staff should provide this support to the campaign. All public relations/media relations programs should flow through the director of university relations.

This official usually needs a staff dedicated to developing campaign communications programs. Internal and external publications along with press releases, campaign publications, and media support require an office devoted to these functions exclusively. There is no reason, however, that these functions should not report through a director of university relations. The director is presumably an expert in dealing with the public and the media and should be able to provide important direction and leadership to the campaign. Precampaign publicity should be initiated by the director of university relations, and a precampaign publicity plan that leads to the ultimate announcement of the campaign should be created and proposed by the director of university relations. Not to involve the chief public relations officer will only lead to hurt feelings and less-than-satisfactory relationships among advancement personnel.

Proposed Campaign Organization

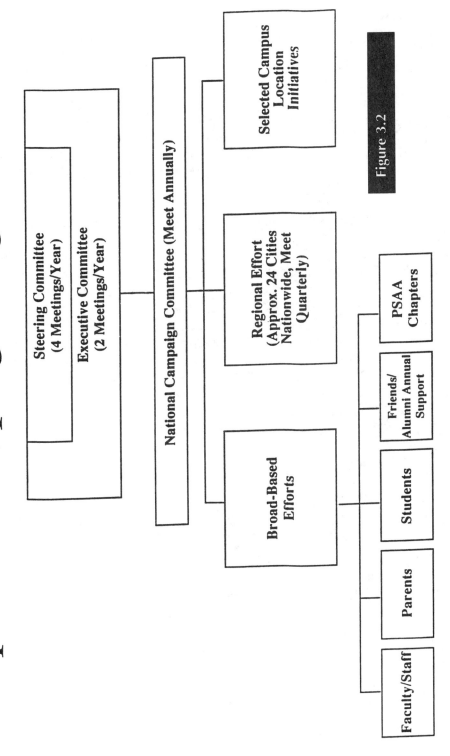

Figure 3.2

Notes

1. M. D. Richards, G. R. Sherratt, "Institutional Advancement Strategies in Hard Times," in *ERIC Report Number 2*. (Washington, DC: American Association of Higher Education, 1981).

2. G. David Gearhart, "A Study of the Relationship Between the Preparation for and Initiation of a Capital Fund-Raising Campaign in a Major Research University and Two Types of Organizational Structure." Ed.D. diss., University of Arkansas, Fayetteville, Arkansas. 1989.

3. G. David Gearhart, M. Bezilla, "Fund Raising Success Takes Teamwork," in *Fund Raising Management*. (March, 1991), pp. 42–44, 46.

4. Rita Bornstein, "The Capital Campaign: Benefits and Hazards," in James L. Fisher and G. H. Quehl ed., *The President and Fund Raising*. (New York: American Council on Education and Macmillan Publishing Company, 1989), pp. 203–204.

5. Paul E. Wisdom, "Another Look at Costs," in James L. Fisher and G. H. Quehl, *The President and Fund Raising*. (New York: American Council on Education and Macmillan Publishing Company, 1989), pp. 147–159.

6. Sharon L. Coldren, *The Constant Quest: Raising Billions Through Capital Campaigns*. (Washington, DC: American Council on Education, 1982), p. 60.

7. Jon Van Til and Associates, *Critical Issues in American Philanthropy: Strengthening Theory and Practice*. (San Francisco: Jossey-Bass Inc., 1990), p. 59.

8. James L. Fisher, G. H. Quehl, ed. *The President and Fund Raising*. (New York: American Council on Education and Macmillan Publishing Company, 1989), p. ix.

FOUR

Volunteers and External Organization

Development literature is full of articles, books, monographs, dissertations, and other materials on the use of volunteers in philanthropic endeavors. Much of the literature discusses the essential role of volunteers in fund raising.[1] Volunteers are extremely important in a capital campaign, especially in securing major gifts. Although staff, including the president, vice presidents, deans, and development officers, can be successful in major gift fund raising without volunteers, it is more likely that the process of solicitation will be accelerated with the strategic involvement of key volunteers.[2]

Uses of Volunteers

Volunteers have many uses during a capital campaign. Some of the more important ones are the following.

Serving in Leadership Capacities as Officers of the Campaign

Depending on the size and scope of the campaign, there may be opportunities for volunteers to serve in a variety of official roles, such as campaign chairperson, vice chairperson, secretary, and treasurer. Numerous committees and task forces throughout the life of the campaign require volunteer leadership, many of which are described in the following pages.

Soliciting Major Gifts

Often a volunteer can make a difference in the solicitation of a major gift. Peer pressure (described in more detail in chapter 5) can be an important factor in closing on a major gift opportunity. Volunteers accompanying staff, particularly the president or vice president for development, can be a powerful team that might leverage a gift that otherwise would not be forthcoming.

Providing Leadership

Volunteers can provide leadership and expertise on organizational and strategic issues relating to gift accounting principles, campaign timing, and campaign promotional materials.

Serving as Spokespeople for the Campaign

Volunteers, along with the president of the institution, can serve as spokespeople with the news media and the institution's constituencies. Many times, volunteers will carry more clout than staff in a community and can serve in an important communications capacity.

Ask only the most dedicated, committed, and energetic volunteers to participate in the volunteer role during the capital campaign. Choose only those volunteers who have interest in supporting the campaign through their own philanthropy. Prepare them to commit their own resources to the effort before they can ask others to do so.

In most cases, volunteers will require extensive training in the solicitation process. This process is outlined in chapter 5.

Regardless of the size of the institution or of the capital campaign, the use of volunteers demands extensive staff time. Volunteers expect the campaign office to tend to their needs and answer their questions, and this expectation should be anticipated. Volunteers are a most valuable resource, and staff members must treat them with care and respect. The "care and feeding" of volunteers during a capital campaign is one of the most important staff assignments, and staff should be prepared to spend many hours in this process.

Barbara Snelling states:

> No matter what the role of its volunteer, the volunteer's gift of
> time should be respected by the professional. There is a respon-

sibility to see that this gift is cherished, not wasted or abused. The stewardship of the volunteer's time is analogous to, and should be taken as seriously as, the stewardship of a voluntary gift of money in which considerable care is given to ensure that the money is managed well and used only for specified purposes.[3]

Recruiting Volunteers

All volunteers, regardless of the level of assignment, will require recruitment. Whenever possible, volunteers should be recruited by the most senior staff. In most cases, this will be the president of the institution and/or the chief development officer, and this action will help to identify the campaign as an important activity. If an executive at a lesser level is sent to recruit possible volunteers, they are likely to dismiss the campaign as unimportant and an unnecessary expenditure of their time.

The recruitment of the senior volunteer leadership must also involve the campaign chairperson, reflecting a unified effort of both administration and alumni and friends. This places the priority of the campaign at the highest level and is an undeniable institutional demonstration of commitment. As Kent E. Dove states,

> Recruitment of volunteers is a shared responsibility and is usually done most successfully from the top down. The campaign chair should be recruited by the top people in an organization . . . the institution should not send in a low-level manager to ask for a commitment. Send top guns—the chief executive officer and the board chair.[4]

The senior development officer in charge of the campaign accompanies the president and chairperson of the campaign throughout the recruitment process. This staff member will have day-to-day contact with the lead volunteers, and a close working relationship from the beginning is very important.

In larger campaigns with multiple committees and assignments, it may not be practical for the president of the university and the chairperson of the campaign to recruit volunteers past the major lead campaign committee. It may be necessary for volunteers and other staff to recruit lower-level campaign committees. This is acceptable provided the recruiters have a full understanding of campaign priorities, volunteer duties, and responsibilities. Sending mixed messages into the volunteer workforce can have a long-lasting and debilitating impact on early campaign planning and objectives.

Ultimately, the volunteer leadership must take ownership of the campaign and make it their campaign. Every facet of the effort must have the support and encouragement of the volunteer structure.

An important first step for volunteers is to make their own commitment to the campaign, particularly as they begin soliciting others for commitments. Many experts in the field insist that volunteers be solicited even before they are asked to serve on major campaign committees. The thought is that a volunteer will be only as good as his or her commitment to the campaign. If a volunteer commits at a lower level than is appropriate for his gift capacity, then it is likely that his volunteer work will be similarly unimpressive.[5]

The theory here seems solid and is difficult to contradict. However, from a practical standpoint, particularly in the first major campaign at a college or university, soliciting volunteers before they are heavily involved in the campaign and before they have experienced working with fellow campaign leaders may be a mistake. Experience has shown that volunteers who have the potential to make major commitments to the institution are more apt to do so only after they are fully entrenched in the campaign and have been convinced that it is an extremely worthwhile effort. Winning a volunteer's complete confidence early on in the process may not be possible. A better tactic might be to inform volunteers that they will be called upon for a "major commitment" at an appropriate time during the campaign. Tell volunteers that a gift request will be forthcoming early in the campaign and that a gift of six or seven figures will be expected if the volunteer joins the national campaign committee.

This, of course, opens up the possibility of preemptive gifts, so the solicitation should not be delayed for too long. However, rushing in with a proposal at the same time the volunteer is being recruited for committee membership may be premature and result in a much smaller commitment than originally desired.

The Campaign Volunteer Committees and Organizational Models

There are numerous ways to organize a volunteer structure for a capital campaign. Practically every capital campaign, however, needs a lead campaign committee or, as it is often termed, the national campaign committee.

The National Campaign Committee

This is the group of volunteers that has been recruited by the president of the institution, chief development officer, and chairperson of the campaign to guide and lead the overall effort. This committee is generally composed of alumni and friends of the institution who are interested in giving their time and talent as well as making a major financial commitment.

In larger institutions, the committee may be representative of campuses, academic branches, and other units. This approach is not necessarily recommended, as an institution should be looking for the most capable and financially viable volunteers without regard to which units are represented. It is more important to have a cohesive volunteer committee composed of individuals who have the ability and wherewithal to be at the same general giving level as their fellow committee members. Committee members who do not have the financial ability to make major commitments to the campaign might feel embarrassed or even inadequate in their committee membership. Most committee members, therefore, should be of sufficient philanthropic ability so that their level of gift support will not be embarrassing or seem inadequate when compared with other committee members.

The size of the national campaign committee will depend a great deal on the institution's constituency. Larger, more complex institutions will often find it necessary to expand the number of committee members. The recent Campaign for Penn State had a total committee membership of 32. Some campaign committees of smaller institutions might find it adequate to hold committee membership to no more than 10 or 15 members. The committee must be small enough so that each member becomes acquainted with his or her fellow committee members, and the national committee becomes a team effort and a special group of supporters working toward a common goal.

The national campaign committee should meet at least four times a year during the life of the campaign. It is necessary to stay in close contact with committee members, and after solicitation assignments have been made, it will be important for committee members to make regular interim reports on a continuing basis. Committee members ought to feel a sense of obligation to get their committee assignments accomplished, knowing that they will be called upon on a quarterly basis to make appropriate reports.

The National Campaign Executive Committee

Depending on the size of the national campaign committee, it may be necessary to create a smaller working group that can meet on a monthly basis. The planning group could consist of the officers of the campaign and appropriate staff members. The planning group guides the campaign on a regular basis and serves as a sounding board for major campaign decisions. The executive committee should have the authority to act on behalf of the national campaign committee.

The Honorary Campaign Committee

There will be alumni and friends of the institution who may want to participate in some way with campaign objectives but are unable to do so because of physical impairments and other considerations. These alumni and friends might be unable to travel and participate in campaign meetings. This honorary status will keep them involved and informed about campaign progress and will serve as a way to recognize a distinct group of benefactors who are interested in the institution but can no longer participate on a regular basis. The honorary committee is also a mechanism to recognize government officials and other friends of the institution whose time is at a premium and who are unable to appropriate the hours necessary for the campaign.

Organizational Models

Several different organizational models exist for the creation of volunteer committees for a capital campaign. It is most important to keep in mind that every committee within the campaign should have a definitive goal and set of objectives. These goals may fluctuate throughout the life of the campaign, but volunteers have to know specifically what is expected of their respective committees. Every volunteer should be given a task plan and a definitive list of prospects and assignments.

Keep in mind, too, that the campaign committee should not be recruited until there are definitive plans and tasks for assignment to those committees. Campaign committees should not be impaneled and organized until the campaign has reached the point where there are goals and objectives for that respective committee. Organizing committees without specific tasks will only lead to confusion. Volunteers will feel the campaign is not progressing and that they have been asked to participate but given no duties or responsibilities. Refrain from organizing committees that do not have task plans. There are few situations worse than a committee that has no purpose for existence.

Many campaigns operate subcommittees under the overall national campaign committee. This provides many advantages in that it allows staff to focus on a defined committee membership and allows for optimum management of the volunteer structure. Organizing the national campaign committee into geographic regions, gift levels, and functional areas helps to maintain a tightly controlled organizational structure and can assist institutions both large and small in moving the effort forward rapidly. However, multiple committees outside the national campaign committee can also lead to confusion and unnecessary dispersement of staff.

Decide early in the campaign how to organize the volunteer committee structure. Volunteers must be able to understand where their committee assignment fits into the overall organizational structure of the campaign, and this structure must be both explainable and defensible to alumni and friends. An organizational structure that is confusing and overly complex wastes staff time. Maintain a tightly controlled committee structure and avoid creating a plethora of committees and subcommittees.

The following are organizational structures and models that commonly exist in capital campaigns. Keep in mind that many campaigns across the country use bits and pieces of each model, and there does not seem to be any clear, definable committee structure that can be recommended as the paradigm.

Gift Level Model

This model creates committees according to gift size. Solicitations are performed sequentially, with the largest gifts solicited first and then down the ladder until the annual fund level has been reached and achieved. These committees are based solely on gift size and do not take into consideration the type of prospect being solicited (i.e., corporate, individual, foundation). Four distinct committee types are prevalent in this model.

Advance Gifts Committee. Its members participate at the highest gift level, soliciting commitments in the advanced stages of the campaign at the $250,000 level and above. This committee must be in place several months—or even years—prior to the public announcement of the campaign, and is responsible for seeking the largest gifts in the campaign from the most generous and influential alumni and friends of the institution. Generally, this committee is composed of a small group of mega-gift benefactors who can solicit their peers at the highest possible level.

This committee will operate throughout the life of the campaign.

Leadership Gifts Committee. Its responsibility is to seek gifts from the volunteer leadership of the campaign. This committee should solicit every member of the national campaign committee as well as other campaign committees, as organized. The leadership gifts committee can broaden its responsibility to solicit the governing board of the institution as well as other significant advisory boards. The committee is so named because it is soliciting commitments from the leadership volunteers of the institution. Campaign leaders must show strong support by donating their own personal resources, and this committee is charged with the responsibility of ferreting out these gifts. This committee's work should be completed prior to the public announcement of the campaign. Development officers should expect 100 percent participation from national campaign committee members.

Major Gifts Committee. This committee is charged with seeking gifts that typically fall below the advance gifts phase, perhaps at the level of $50,000 to $100,000 and above, and its work can continue throughout the life of the campaign. It is possible to merge this committee with the advance gifts committee or to redefine its mission and objectives as the campaign moves forward out of the advance gift phase.

Annual Fund Committee. As noted previously, it is important to continue the annual fund component of the development program, even during the life of a capital campaign. Many people who are alumni and friends of the institution do not have the wherewithal to make a major capital campaign gift but will continue to give annually to the institution. This committee must not seek preemptive gifts from individuals who do have the capacity to make larger capital commitments over a multiyear period. However, alumni who cannot make major commitments will still want to be involved in the campaign and will want to do their part by making an annual gift. A committee organized to deal with this level of giving is important to the overall welfare of the campaign.

Functional Model

Many campaigns are organized around functional models rather than gift levels. Again, it is possible to organize a campaign using both a gift model and a functional model. The functional model, unlike the gift model, concentrates on the origin of the gift. In other words, is an alumnus, friend, corporation, or foundation making the commitment? Is it a planned, irrevocable gift or an annual gift? This model is not necessarily concerned with the dollar level of a particular solicitation, but rather with the entity that is making the commitment. Three committee types are represented in this model.

Corporate and Foundation Gifts Committee. This committee is charged with the responsibility of soliciting gifts from corporations and foundations. Although the committee should be concerned with gift levels and soliciting gifts sequentially, its main concern is to concentrate on the functional area of corporations and foundations. Take care to recruit candidates who are knowledgeable about corporate and foundation giving, as well as those who have real or perceived clout in the corporate community. Many times the entire national campaign committee serves in the capacity of the corporate and foundation committee, allowing for maximum input from all committee members. Throughout the life of The Campaign for Penn State, a separate corporate and foundation committee was not used. The belief was that the committee of the whole (The National Campaign Committee) should concentrate on foundations and corporations. Staff could then draw from the expertise and knowledge of all committee members rather than rely on the knowledge of a few serving on a separate committee. The advantage of a separate committee is that it allows a group of specially qualified volunteers to concentrate on the corporate and foundation sphere. Those volunteers should keep in mind that much expertise will exist among other national campaign committee members not serving on this committee.

Individual Gifts Committee. As the name implies, this committee focuses on individual alumni and friends.

Irrevocable Planned Gifts Committee. It is unusual to find this committee in the organizational structure of a capital campaign. Committee members concentrate on irrevocable gifts such as estate notes, charitable remainder trusts, pooled income funds, gift annuities, and other gifts that require special expertise and knowledge. There is likely to be great overlap between this committee and the individual gifts committee, as volunteers have no way of knowing when an individual may want to use a deferred-giving technique. Organizing a separate committee for this purpose might be confusing to volunteers in the solicitation process and is not recommended.

Annual Fund Committee. This group can be organized either from a gift standpoint or functional standpoint. Most institutions have some form of annual giving program, and this committee would seek to keep in place certain annual fund efforts during the life of the capital campaign. Keep in mind that preemptive gifts are often made when annual fund committees are in place, and great care should be taken to keep these types of gifts to a minimum. It may be necessary to form this committee in the final stages of the campaign and use it as a "cleanup crew," more concerned with numbers of gifts rather than the size of contributions.

Geographic Model

Those institutions with large constituencies in multiple locations may want to consider a geographic model that creates volunteer committees on either a regional or city basis. One advantage of the geographic model is that it uses volunteers to make calls on prospects living in their local areas. Robert L. Krit feels that this enhances the solicitation process because prospects "are more likely to respond to contacts made by local solicitors."[6]

- **Regional Committees.** For those institutions that wish to cover the entire continental United States, development officers may want to consider creating multiple geographic regional committees. Nevertheless, regions can be so large that the area is cumbersome and unmanageable and, thus, impractical when attempting to solicit major gift prospects. Regional volunteer chairpersons should be within a 200-mile radius of any major gift solicitation they may be involved in. If the region spreads out much further, it is not likely that the chairperson will make the solicitation.

  Managing a large network of committees with multiple volunteers in numerous regions and cities requires a tremendous amount of staff time and follow-up and can be a very difficult process.

- **Major City Committees.** Perhaps one compromise to the regional approach is to organize geographic volunteer committees in major cities. This strategy would create a volunteer chairperson and committee in each of the major cities across the continental United States. This model, of course, will not cover every prospect, but it will give the campaign a sense of national breadth and scope.

Academic Unit Model

Institutions may want to consider creating volunteer committees by academic unit. For large multicampus institutions, this model is built around campuses, departments, and schools of study, and volunteers are organized into committees for each of these academic units. Thus, the department of engineering has its own volunteer campaign committee, as does the department of business, the department of liberal arts, and so on. For small institutions, committees can be organized around departments or academic divisions.

While this model has the advantage of bringing together an institution's total constituency, it tends to be unwieldy and unmanageable. The model also tends to break down the campaign into competing fiefdoms and does not allow for a cohesive, systematic approach to fund raising. The campaign becomes a series of multiple campaigns, rather than a unilateral approach that promotes the entire university toward common objectives.

Communications Committee

The committees discussed thus far are designed to be involved in the solicitation, cultivation, and research of prospects. It is often necessary to form other committees that do not have solicitation and cultivation goals. One such committee is the communications committee.

Many institutions have alumni in the communications field who can provide expertise, support, and advice to a campaign's communications program.

Most campaigns pick and choose from each of these models and create an organizational structure that seems right for that particular college or university. These models should not be looked upon as mutually exclusive, and campaigns normally blend all of the models in an attempt to form the best possible organizational structure.

Role of the Campaign Chairperson

The national campaign chairperson is in a critically important position, and an individual should be tapped to fill this role early on in the campaign planning. As Robert L. Krit writes, "obviously, [the campaign chair] should be someone who holds a high position in the business or social life of the community, but this in itself is not sufficient. The general chairperson must have the willingness and the time to work. A prominent name on a letterhead alone will not attract support."[7]

Most likely, the individual will be an alumnus of the institution, but this is not absolutely required. It is advisable, however, because an institution wants its alumni to identify closely with a successful alumnus who is heading up the campaign.

There are many elements that come together to create the ultimate campaign chairperson. The following are some positions worth consideration when looking for a candidate.

- **The Chairperson, President, or Chief Executive Officer of a Nationally Respected Company.** An individual with these credentials will be immediately recognized by alumni and friends of the institution and will have instant clout when calling on prospects. The CEO of a major company also has staff available to him or her to assist in a multitude of campaign arrangements. Often the CEO can use corporate transportation when coupled with a business trip.
- **A Retired CEO of a Major Company.** Often these individuals make excellent campaign chairpersons. However, an institution must keep in mind that a CEO's clout is diminished at retirement, and even though the individual may have time to give to the campaign, he or she may have diminished leverage with major gift prospects.
- **Professionals.** Doctors, lawyers, engineers, accountants, money managers, and financial managers all can make good campaign chairpersons provided they are willing to devote the time and effort to the process. Many professionals simply cannot appropriate the time necessary to the task.

Some important characteristics to look for when seeking the right candidate follow:

- **Speaking Ability.** The chairperson of the campaign should have extraordinarily good public speaking ability. He or she will be called upon countless times in large group settings, and for all intents will be the spokesperson for the campaign. The ideal is an individual who is at ease with the microphone as well as comfortable in responding to tough questions from the news media.
- **Affable and Ingratiating.** The campaign chairperson should be an individual who is liked and respected by fellow committee members. The chairperson must be a true leader, some-

one that other committee members want to follow. The committee chairperson can be a hard driver, but this must be tempered with an ingratiating style that is contagious among other committee members.

The national campaign chairperson should be a person who stimulates interest and enthusiasm for the entire project. His or her time and effort must be devoted to policy decisions and the cultivation and negotiation of major commitments to the campaign. The chairperson helps to inspire and persuade members of the national campaign committee to carry out their responsibilities thoroughly and promptly.

The national campaign chairperson:

- has executive responsibility for the successful completion of the campaign;
- presides at all meetings of the national campaign committee and the executive committee and is involved in every aspect of the planning and implementation of campaign objectives;
- reports progress to the governing board of the institution as well as to campaign support groups;
- endorses and represents the campaign goals and plans and is the primary spokesperson for the campaign;
- speaks publicly on the campaign's behalf to the media and to the institution's various constituencies; and
- is heavily involved in the leadership phase of the campaign in soliciting major gifts for the effort.

In short, the campaign chairperson must appropriate enormous energy and enthusiasm and must dedicate himself or herself to leading the campaign throughout its life. Penn State was blessed with the ultimate campaign chairperson in William A. Schreyer, former chairman and CEO of Merrill Lynch. He provided almost daily leadership and enthusiastic support to the campaign. He was pivotal in its success.

Role of the Campaign Vice Chairperson

Use of the title campaign vice chairperson is a way to elevate certain committee members to special status. Also, it is important to have at least one vice chairperson who can fill in from time to time for the campaign chairperson.

A campaign vice chairperson can serve as chairperson of major campaign committees. In The Campaign for Penn State, Joe Paterno, nationally acclaimed football coach, served as one of three vice chairpersons. His leadership and support was a major reason for the campaign's success.

Role of the Campaign Treasurer

This position, if occupied by a volunteer, may be mostly ceremonial. Treasurer's reports are generally created by campaign staff, but the campaign treasurer should deliver these reports at all campaign meetings.

A good campaign treasurer will want to become enmeshed in the various development office reports that are published regularly. The treasurer should monitor these reports, being concerned with both the dollars raised for the campaign as well as the percentage of the needs statement that is being funded.

Role of the Governing Board

The role of the governing board depends on the type of institution that is conducting a capital campaign.

The governing board of an independent institution is often staffed with individuals who have the potential to make major philanthropic commitments to the institution. In this case, the board may be an excellent source of campaign committee members, and the use of governing board members on a capital campaign committee is advisable. If governing board representatives serve in this capacity, it will heighten the awareness, interest, and importance of the campaign among the governing board members.

In public institutions the governing board is often formed through political appointments, and the board members may have little or no interest in philanthropic endeavors.

In either case, the governing board ought to show full support of the fund-raising effort by endorsing it with a board resolution early in the public phase of the campaign. Obviously, the president of the institution will want to keep the governing board fully apprised of campaign objectives, but at some point in the early stages of the campaign, it is advisable to ask the governing board to formally endorse the effort (see sample endorsement in appendix F).

Role of the Development Council/ Foundation Board

Many institutions already have volunteer organizations in place prior to the launching of a capital campaign. These organizations may be titled development councils, boards of visitors, development advisory boards, or perhaps even foundation boards. In large public universities, the foundation board may have legal authority over gift assets to the institution. The foundation board may operate as a development governing board, and the chief executive officer of the foundation is often the chief development officer of the institution. These are legal entities created by the institution to serve as conduits for private gifts, and many of them have grown to be powerful organizations that literally guide and direct all aspects of the development program. The foundation board may, indeed, be the unit that gives authority to a national campaign committee, but rarely does this foundation board actually become the national committee.

Development councils and boards may, in fact, conflict with a national campaign committee, and care should be taken to be certain that there is a clear delineation of responsibilities among these various constituency units.

An advisory development board or council may coexist with a national campaign committee, or an institution may decide to put the council on hold during the life of the capital campaign. It will be difficult for staff to service both entities during a campaign, and a development council that is seeking private gift support for the institution may simply be superfluous during the years of a capital campaign if another entity has been formed. This will be a difficult choice for an institution but one that must be thought out in advance.

The Faculty/Staff Component

Any good campaign plan, regardless of the size of the institution, will have a faculty/staff component.

Although some experts claim that faculty/staff giving to a capital campaign increases the likelihood of corporate and foundation support to the institution, this has not been proven. There are some foundations that are interested in faculty and staff giving, but, in general, this does not seem to be a major concern among corporations and most foundations.

On the other hand, faculty and staff giving is important to "ignite" positive feelings on campus among faculty and student groups. Much positive publicity should surround a faculty/staff campaign to heighten awareness of the capital campaign in general.

A faculty/staff campaign should occur toward the middle of the overall campaign and can serve as a catalyst to reinvigorate the effort. There are a multitude of ways to solicit faculty and staff, but only two will be dealt with here.

Program-Specific Solicitation

Many institutions choose an all-university need that might appeal to a large number of faculty and staff members—renovation of the library, or the creation of faculty fellowships or student scholarships. Faculty and staff are then asked to contribute to this need each year for the life of the campaign. Many times a multiyear pledge is requested, and faculty and staff are solicited by their peers during a defined period of one to two months.

The disadvantage of this method is that it does not allow faculty and staff to designate their giving toward a particular entity or discipline of their choice. In other words, a professor of biology may want to contribute to the biology department or to the college of his or her choice. Program-specific fund raising does not promote this kind of activity.

Annual Program Designation

The preferred method of solicitation of faculty and staff, particularly at major universities with multiple campuses and schools of study, is to allow faculty and staff to designate their giving on an annual basis to an entity of their choice. A multiyear pledge is still possible, or the institution can simply solicit faculty and staff annually throughout the life of the campaign. If annual solicitation is to take place, then major gift prospects among faculty and staff (there may, in fact, be some) should take place long before the faculty and staff campaign. Faculty and staff campaigns are notorious for preemptive gifts from individuals who have the means to contribute a much larger pledge.

The Student Component

The student component can also galvanize a campaign. Although resources garnered by such a campaign may be minimal, the public relations value of this effort can be extremely important.

The student campaign is probably best organized around living units where competition between these units can be attained. An alternative is the use of student clubs and organizations. Students will likely want to rally around a particular campaign need, and they should be given the opportunity to choose one that will directly benefit them.

Because of the matriculation of students, the student campaign should be held on an annual basis throughout the life of the overall capital campaign. This will help to alleviate the problems of student continuity but, on the other hand, will create problems of training and deployment of student volunteers.

The Local Community Component

This is an opportunity for smaller businesses, associations, and other entities in the region surrounding the institution to participate in the campaign by making a pledge commitment. A community-based campaign should not run throughout the life of the capital campaign, but rather have a defined window of solicitation that might occupy a three- or six-month period of time. Volunteers are recruited to solicit local businesses and associations for five-year pledges. This campaign uses a lot of volunteers, as targeted businesses and associations are divided among multiple solicitors. The solicitation effort would begin with training sessions and division of responsibilities and prospects. Volunteers would be given a definitive period of time in which to make their solicitations and then report back at the end of that period.

The community campaign is another way to galvanize support in the local area. Generally, this campaign gains small contributions, of an annual type.

This campaign should not be inaugurated until the advance and major gift phases have taken care of all of the major gift opportunities in that region. There may, in fact, be some major commitments that could be forthcoming, and these prospects should have already been contacted and proposals presented to them long before a community campaign is launched. This will help to ensure that preemptive gifts are not made.

The three efforts described above, the faculty/staff component, the student component, and the local community component, all have similar objectives. They are targeted toward a specific populace; they have, as one of their objectives, the garnering of support from a large group of contributors at a low level; and, finally, they can produce extraordinarily favorable publicity for a campaign.

All three of these efforts should be given to the same development staff. Depending on the size and scope of the annual fund staff, these three campaigns might fit well into the annual giving program during a capital campaign. The process will require staff time, and some workers may question the validity of the campaigns when considering the dollar return on staff investment. Nevertheless, these campaign efforts are important and should be considered.

The Alumni Association During the Capital Campaign

Most colleges and universities have alumni offices that may be associated with the development program but are separate and distinct entities, not necessarily involved with fund raising.

These alumni offices may take the form of separate legal entities with private governing boards. In some smaller independent institutions, the alumni office is governed entirely by the institution, and the separate alumni association board serves in an advisory capacity to the institution.

Regardless of the type of alumni association at a particular college or university, there will be a need to determine how to use an alumni support group, alumni association, or alumni office during the capital campaign. The use of the alumni association or alumni office will depend greatly on the organizational structure of that entity. Some suggested uses follow.

■ Invite the alumni association to pass a resolution in support of the capital campaign.

- Invite the alumni association to fund a particular identified project within the capital campaign such as a scholarship, fellowship, or even an endowed chair. Support for this project could come from the association's own assets. Campaign staff should be careful that the association does not present a conflict of solicitation of alumni in an effort to fulfill its own campaign commitment.
- If the alumni entity has clubs in certain geographic areas, these clubs can serve as excellent vehicles for a public relations program about the campaign. Ask that the clubs allow campaign volunteers and staff to speak before club programs, informing the alumni about the campaign and its objectives.
- Alumni clubs can also sponsor individual scholarships from their particular geographic regions. Funds for these scholarships can be generated through dues or a variety of other techniques.

Keeping the alumni association and alumni office involved in campaign planning is important in the early stages of the campaign. Potential conflict between the association objectives and the capital campaign should be avoided, and this will only be possible through open communication and coordination.

Athletic Fund Raising During the Capital Campaign

For the most part, athletic fund raising at colleges and universities consists of ticket options and membership in booster club organizations. These programs generally do not interfere with the ongoing process of development for academic programs and are not part of the ongoing development program of a college or university.

There are a handful of institutions, however, that have begun major gift fund-raising programs in athletics, some of which are designed to endow positions within the athletic department, including athletic team positions such as quarterback, center, guard, tackle, and so on. One institution that has managed this process with success is the University of Southern California.[8]

In large complex universities with nationally recognized athletic programs, the needs statement of the capital campaign should include a component for the athletic department. Athletic fund raising is becoming more and more sophisticated, and institutions would be wise to build upon alumni interest rather than exclude the program from the capital campaign.

The Capital Campaign and Parent Giving

Many colleges and universities regularly solicit parents for contributions to the institution. Often, this is conducted through an institution's annual giving program and may include a phone or mail campaign.

During a capital campaign, an institution should not ignore the potential of major gifts from the parent population. Parents who have been contributing to the annual fund regularly would be prime prospects for capital gifts at higher levels, and these prospects should be treated as any other major gift prospect.

Some institutions have chosen to isolate parents, and to appeal to them separately during the capital campaign. While this is certainly possible from an organizational standpoint, it may simply garner smaller commitments of an annual fund nature. It is probably best to treat this group as any other university constituency and solicit those parents that might have the potential to make major gifts to the capital campaign.

Notes

1. Barbara Snelling, "Recruiting, Training, and Managing Volunteers," in A. Westley Rowland, ed., *Handbook of Institutional Advancement: A Modern Guide to Executive Management, Institutional Relations, Fund-Raising, Alumni Relations, Publications, Periodicals, and Enrollment 2nd ed.* (San Francisco: Jossey-Bass Inc., 1990), pp. 67–77.
2. Margaret A. Duronio, B.A. Loessin, *Effective Fund Raising in Higher Education: Ten Success Stories.* (San Francisco: Jossey-Bass Inc., 1991), p. 214.
3. Snelling, "Recruiting, Training, and Managing Volunteers," in *Handbook of Institutional Advancement: A Modern Guide to Executive Management, Institutional Relations, Fund-Raising, Alumni Relations, Publications, Periodicals, and Enrollment 2nd ed.*, p. 70.
4. Kent E. Dove, *Conducting a Successful Capital Campaign: A Com-*

prehensive Guide for Nonprofit Organizations. (San Francisco: Jossey-Bass Inc., 1988), pp. 44, 45.

5. Richard Fox, "Your Partnership with Power People," *CASE CURRENTS vol. x no. 20.* (November/December 1984): 43.
6. Robert L. Krit, *The Fund-Raising Handbook.* (The United States of America: Scott Foresman Professional Books, 1991), p. 13.
7. Krit, *The Fund-Raising Handbook,* p. 35.
8. Gary Smith, "That Old School Spirit: C. Elerding Endows USC Football Team's Coach and Punter," in *Sports Illustrated vol. 69.* (November 28, 1988): 110–114.

FIVE

Solicitation Process— Asking for the Gift

Soliciting a major gift—$100,000 or more—is not a single act, but rather a process. The cultivation and solicitation of alumni, friends, corporations, foundations, and associations is a careful step-by-step endeavor that culminates in convincing the benefactor that his or her support is critical. This can take months and even years of planning to bring to fruition. Rarely, if ever, is a major gift made to an institution without careful and deliberate planning by volunteers and staff. "Instantaneous gifts" that surprise both the development officer and the institution are rare and indeed seldom realized.

Why People Give to Capital Campaigns

Although many considerations can enter the mind of a philanthropist who is considering a major gift, here are the most common:

Tax Considerations

Ever since Congress enacted income and estate taxes, the American people have been concerned about reducing their tax burden.

As Jon Van Til and Associates points out, the reason the federal government provides tax deductions for philanthropic gifts is twofold. One, the government feels the services provided by not-for-profit organizations actually relieve the government of a burden. Second, a philanthropic gift does not "enrich" the benefactor.[1]

While Congress has continued to reduce the tax advantages of charitable giving, substantial benefits can still be realized by individuals who itemize deductions of contributions made to qualifying organizations.[2]

The tax advantages of charitable giving differ according to the types of gifts made to an institution. The following are some examples of such gifts.

Gifts of Cash. The simplest way to make a gift to a college or university is to give cash. The date of the gift is the date that the check is mailed or delivered. Gifts of cash may be deducted up to 50 percent of adjusted gross income, with a five-year carryover for any excess.

Gifts of Appreciated Property. If an institution sells long-term property—that is, property that it has owned for more than one year—that institution is liable for capital gains tax on any appreciation. However, if an institution makes a gift of this property to a qualifying charitable organization, it may avoid any tax liability on that appreciation. Institutions are also allowed a charitable deduction for the fair market value of the property that is transferred. (The cost basis must be used for gifts of property held for one year or less.)

Gifts of long-term, appreciated property are deductible up to 30 percent of adjusted gross income, with a five-year carryover for any excess. An individual may elect to have the contribution of such property come under the 50 percent limit by reducing the total allowable contribution to the cost basis. Such an election may be warranted if the total appreciation is small.

Tangible Personal Property. A charitable deduction is allowed for a gift of tangible, personal property—for example, artwork, books, stamp collections, and manuscripts. Tax regulations affecting such gifts held more than one year by the donor depend in part on how the gift will be used. If a university accepts a painting for its permanent collection, for example—a related use—the donor can claim a charitable deduction for the fair market value of that property and may deduct up to 30 percent of the adjusted gross income in the year of the gift.

If the gift is put to an unrelated use by the university—(e.g., a stamp collection given to the college of science to sell for use of proceeds)—the donor's deduction is limited to the cost basis, which may be deducted up to 50 percent of adjusted gross income in the year of the gift.

The five-year carryover may be used for any excess above the prescribed limits. Strict valuation and reporting requirements apply to gifts of appreciated property, depending upon the type of property given and the charitable deduction claimed.

Bargain Sales. When property is sold to the university for less than its fair market value, the transaction is called a bargain sale. The difference between the fair market value and the sale price is deductible as a charitable gift. If the property has a long-term capital gain, the donor is liable for the portion of gain allocable to the selling price.

Gifts of Life Insurance. Life insurance may provide a current and future charitable income tax deduction if the benefactor assigns ownership of the policy to the institution. If the policy is paid up, the deduction is the amount of the replacement value, but not more than the cost basis (usually, the total of all premiums paid less dividends received). If premiums are still being paid, the deduction will be roughly equal to the cash surrender value. Future premium payments also are fully deductible.

Deferred Gifts. To encourage certain individuals to make philanthropic gifts to higher education and to other qualifying organizations, the federal government allows a number of vehicles for making deferred gifts. In essence, a donor can take a substantial charitable deduction now for a gift that the institution will not actually receive until a later date—usually after the death of the donor and selected survivors. The greatest tax benefits of such plans are usually reserved for older individuals.

When a benefactor contributes cash, securities, or real property as deferred gifts, he or she continues receiving income from the property for life, and usually the life of at least one other, such as a spouse. The property is received by the college or university after the death of the last surviving beneficiary.

A person is able to take an income tax deduction in the year of the gift (or transfer) for the value of the property, less the value of the life interest retained. This is often referred to as the remainder value. The amount of the deduction is based on Treasury tables and takes into account the life expectancies of, and expected payments to, all noncharitable beneficiaries.

Deferred-giving instruments include a pooled income fund; charitable gift annuities; charitable remainder trusts, including the charitable remainder unitrust and charitable remainder annuity trust; charitable lead trust; and a gift of remainder interest in a home or farm.

Peer Pressure

The old adage, "People give to people," should be embedded in the minds of all development officers. The whole concept of volunteerism is built around the premise that one's peers are more successful in soliciting a gift from friends and associates than a disassociated third party. A recent survey of 10 American public and independent research universities involved in capital campaigns indicated that volunteers play a critical role in asking for and securing major gifts of six figures and above.[3]

A CEO of a Fortune 500 company recently turned down the request of a community fund-raising organization to head its campaign. The CEO's basic rationale was that she didn't want to be put on her colleagues' lists after she had asked them to support her cause. Human nature is such that it is very difficult to turn down the request of a friend and colleague or business associate. This is not to say that the benefactor would support any cause, regardless of its stated purpose. Certainly, the benefactor must recognize and appreciate the importance of the philanthropic endeavor. But experts in the field have discovered that time and time again, it is the volunteer who can exercise a degree of peer pressure that, when coupled with a sincere and worthy cause for support, will convince a prospect to contribute. Many times the successful solicitation team consists of a lead volunteer and the president or chief executive officer of the institution. Business men and women want to know that their peers and associates are also supporting the endeavor with their gifts. As Kent E. Dove writes,

"There is no substitute for the influence a volunteer can have on certain prospective donors. In many cases, the staffs' influence is negligible compared to that of the right volunteer."[4]

The donor doing what he or she feels is expected can play a part in peer-pressure giving. Many individuals, not wishing to be considered a "low-end" donor, will contribute to an endeavor at the "expected" level. Directors of development are quite often asked the question, "What are others doing for the campaign and what do you expect of me?" Wise development officers use peer pressure to their advantage. Be alert for opportunities in matching the right volunteer to the right prospect.

Altruism

Do not assume that there are hidden agendas and motives for giving money away. Many benefactors genuinely are concerned about the welfare of a particular institution. Philanthropists often are motivated by a sincere desire to help mankind; they are unselfishly concerned for the welfare of others. Major benefactors to colleges and universities hope that their efforts will lead to the improvement and betterment of the institution that they have adopted. According to Jerold Panas, "Large donors give to heroic, exciting programs rather than needy institutions . . . It is trite, but true: an institution must exhibit the audacity and power of an idea whose time has come."[5]

Million-dollar-plus gifts are seldom given on the basis of peer pressure and tax avoidance. Most benefactors at these levels see an opportunity to shape and mold the future of higher education. Indeed, whole colleges and universities have been transformed literally overnight because of the massive infusion of gift dollars.

Immortality

Most people want to be remembered and to make their mark on the world. Most of the time this desire takes the form of raising a healthy family. Children become a reflection of their parents and continue the family traditions.

The quest for immortality also can play an important role in major gift fund raising at colleges and universities. Harvard, Stanford, Rice, Bucknell, and Duke Universities, to name only a few, are all institutions that were named for philanthropists who injected resources into the institution. Endowments at colleges and universities in the last 20 years have increased steadily as a result of major gifts for professorships, chairs, fellowships, and scholarships in perpetuity. Benefactors want to be remembered for this support and are willing to make six- and seven-figure contributions so that their memory is forever intertwined into the academic fabric. Academic institutions are places of wholesome integrity and provide the perfect setting for a donor to "carve out a piece of immortality." Do not mistake a donor's shyness or lack of insistence on naming opportunities as necessarily genuine. Many benefactors do not actively seek publicity. It is the development officer's job to ferret out a donor's real thoughts and inner feelings about perpetual naming opportunities. Perhaps it is not an understatement to say that 90 percent of the time benefactors do want to be recognized, if only modestly, for what they have done to enhance education through their giving. A wise director of development will not give up until he or she is absolutely convinced that the benefactor sincerely wishes anonymity.

Control, Power, and Authority

All seasoned development officers have experienced the problem of benefactors wanting to exercise their authority, power, and control over the institution through their gifts. This desire for influence can range from donors insisting on football tickets on the 50-yard line to others demanding that an entire curriculum be changed. Around March or April, many directors of development become de facto admissions officers, as benefactors attempt to exercise their influence to get their sons and daughters and the sons and daughters of friends and business associates into the institution.

One small, independent, prestigious college in the Midwest completely changed the master plan of the institution because of one donor's insistence. True enough, that one donor pumped millions of dollars into the college, but his thoughts on the physical plant were not always logical or practical. Nevertheless, the administration succumbed to his wishes for fear of angering him and subsequently being excluded from his estate plans. Even today, 10 years after the benefactor's death, the college's president is housed in an old, dilapidated house far removed from the campus administrative core, for no other reason than the fact that this particular benefactor insisted on it.

One also might recall the prestigious institution in the East, where the board of trustees voted to make the college coeducational. A major benefactor emerged with a proposal: "If you remain a women's institution, I will give you $10 million." The college to this day does not accept male students.

Many major benefactors will come to feel an ownership of the institution and will exercise control, power, and authority over the management of the college or university. Their interests may indeed be beneficent, and they may truthfully be philanthropists in every sense of the word, but their interest and their financial support extends much further than a true philanthropic spirit. No worthy institution should compromise its basic integrity for any benefactor, large or small.

A Desire to Be Included, to Belong, to Be Important

Benefactors of all ages and philanthropic levels generally want to be a part of a successful enterprise. In the final months of The Campaign for Penn State, the decisive selling point to donors who had not committed was that this was their last chance to become a part of a very successful endeavor. Those who had held out to the last weeks and months of the campaign finally committed to the effort, realizing that they would be left out and would not be a part of the campaign's grand success.

Many gift programs are designed around gala dinners and other events that list benefactors in programs and brochures. The benefactor is listed by levels according to the degree of support, and the classifications are as broad as the gifts themselves. But individuals will invariably turn to the page where they expect to be listed to be certain that they have been included at the appropriate level. Practically everyone wants to be part of a successful endeavor. Often, it can be the primary motivator for major gift support. Harold J. Seymour stated nearly 30 years ago: "It appears to be a logical corollary—assuming we all aspire to be sought and to be worthwhile members of worthwhile groups—that there can hardly be any stronger motivation for supporting a group or cause than simple pride of association." This still holds true today.[6]

To Change History

Experience has shown that there are a number of wealthy benefactors who desire to change the course of history. When John D.

Rockefeller Jr. was approached about the renovation and restoration of Colonial Williamsburg, he recognized a distinct opportunity to save an important part of the history of this nation. Rockefeller stated many times that all it took was leadership, ingenuity, and lots of money—probably not necessarily in that order.

Andrew Carnegie recognized the importance of building libraries throughout America. His gifts helped to change the course of education in this country—as he knew they would. Time and time again people of privilege, class, and wealth have transformed their dreams into reality through philanthropy. This impulse seems to be on a higher plane than a more ordinary desire to perpetuate one's own memory.

It is true that the age of the Rockefellers, Carnegies, Vanderbilts, and Mellons is long gone. However, philanthropists will continue to build institutions making their vision, idealism, and dreams reality through their giving.

Don't Let the Children Have It

Among wealthier benefactors, there seems to be an emerging trend away from passing great wealth onto one's children. Benefactors have come to realize that great wealth passed on to children can many times have a deleterious effect on the lives of their offspring. Benefactors claim that children who realize that they will inherit $20 million or $30 million have no incentive to live a worthy and disciplined life.[7]

Seventy-five years ago, corporate executives built their wealth much differently than today. One had to invent a better product, own the company outright, or discover oil or gas. Today, however, companies in all sectors are paying huge salaries to ensure longevity of talent among corporate officers. It is not unusual for the chief executive officer of a Fortune 500 company to make anywhere from $2 million to $6 million annually in salary and bonuses. Such an executive will not be able to avoid building an estate of $20 million, $30 million, or even $40 million. The decision of what to do with this estate and to whom to go to for counseling about this important issue will become increasingly more common. The decade of the 1990s and beyond will bring a whole new generation of wealthy individuals who have climbed the corporate ladder and have built sizable estates from salary and other corporate incentives.

All of the Above

Most benefactors exhibit a smattering of all of the above characteristics. When isolated, some of the reasons why people give seem self-centered, egotistical, and not in keeping with the true spirit of the academy. Keep in mind, however, that perhaps none of the reasons cited above are inherently bad. It is important to remember that in the final analysis, no one is *required* to make a gift to a college or university.

Why People Do Not Give to Colleges and Universities

"My Money Is All Tied Up"

During the late 1970s, when inflation was rampant and interest rates climbed to incredible heights, prospects across the country claimed that all of their money was sunk into certificates of deposit. Similarly, many donors proclaim that they are on a fixed income and that their funds are tied up in trusts, certificates of deposit, stocks, and bonds that do not allow for readily accessible cash.

"Where Have You Been All These Years?"

Individuals who graduated from a college or university and then moved to other regions of the country often lose identity with their alma mater. There are, of course, hundreds and hundreds of philanthropic causes, and alumni develop loyalties to a host of community causes over a period of years. When the director of development from their alma mater comes calling, they are likely to ask, "Where have you been all these years?" Many of these people are already giving to the community symphony, the local United Way, and perhaps other colleges and universities in their geographic areas. People tend to give where they live, and for many institutions it may be difficult to regain the loyalty of the prospects. This is a compelling reason for maintaining close ties with alumni as they climb the ladder of success.

"I Am Leaving My Life's Labor to My Children"

Although many major benefactors wish to avoid leaving a substantial estate to their children, often there is the reverse situation.

Many prospects do indeed want to pass their life's labor on to their children; they have worked hard to build a large estate and want their children to live a better life than they had in their early years. They want their children to be untroubled by financial worries.

The Depression Syndrome

Time and time again, campaign officials will encounter prospects who lived through the years of the Great Depression, when they were literally concerned about the next meal on the table. These prospects find it extremely difficult to part with capital, fearing that history will repeat itself, and they will not be able to take care of themselves or their family. This line of thinking is a very real phenomenon that is difficult to overcome.

An elderly prospect at a southwestern land-grant university was cultivated for many years by the president of the institution and the development staff. But she never made a major gift to the institution and died intestate. At the public hearing where her estate was distributed, it was learned that at the time of her death, she possessed more than $13 million in certificates of deposit, bonds, and cash. Her regular passbook checking account had a balance of more than $210,000.

"You'll Stop Coming To See Me"

Many donors actually enjoy the game of "cat and mouse." They thrive on the attention of presidents, development officers, deans, and others visiting them on a regular basis. These donors reason that if they make a major commitment to an institution, the staff will stop coming to see them and simply move on to another prospect. One development director was never so shocked as when a prospect asked him point blank, "If I go ahead and make a gift to your institution, will you still come to see me?" Many donors, especially those in advanced years, enjoy visits by university or college personnel, especially the president or other chief officers of the institution. They are fearful that once they have signed on the dotted line incentive or reason for continued cultivation will no longer exist. This argues for a strong donor recognition program, ensuring benefactors that they will not be forgotten even after their commitment has been secured.

Philanthropy Has Never Been a Habit

Many people have never enjoyed the true spirit of philanthropy as a part of their daily life. They have never been a member of a church where giving is an integral part of belonging. They have never been deeply involved in community causes where they are called upon to support community chests, United Ways, or other philanthropic endeavors. They have not acquired a habit of giving and do not understand the nature or value of giving. Writing out a check for an eleemosynary organization is simply not a part of their lives and may never be. Generosity is a learned behavior and is not necessarily an inherent attribute.

The Pickle Theory

An old adage states, "If you can get the first pickle out of the jar, the rest will follow with relative ease." The same is true with many benefactors. The problem is not that they lack the resources to make a gift to the institution. Rather, they simply cannot comprehend the idea of a dollar leaving their hands.

Taxes

Just as tax considerations can motivate a contribution, they also can have a deleterious effect on giving. While tax rates have risen and fallen through the years, philanthropy has continued to increase steadily. Nevertheless, recent laws related to the alternative minimum tax have unfavorably influenced gifts by donors in high tax brackets.

Physicians and Attorneys as Benefactors

For many years, directors of development throughout the country have been asked the question, "Why don't physicians give to their alma maters?" Actually, there does not appear to be a single statistical analysis that shows that physicians don't give their "fair share." However, statistics aside, many development directors feel strongly that physicians—and for that matter, attorneys—do not make philanthropic gifts. Here are a few possible reasons why these professionals don't contribute.

1. Physicians and lawyers spend an inordinate amount of time studying in college to assure that they are admitted to medical

or law school. The college experience is a serious one for future physicians and lawyers, and many times this experience becomes one of drudgery—a time of working, studying, and praying that they will be good enough to be admitted to a prestigious medical or law school. Premedical and prelaw students, therefore, may not remember these years with affection.

2. Many physicians and attorneys exhibit a great loyalty to their medical school or law school and not their undergraduate experience. Professional institutions can usurp loyalty to undergraduate institutions because medical or law school experience is so important, difficult, and totally consuming. Alumni are bonded to those institutions rather than their undergraduate experience.

3. Many physicians and attorneys believe that they are already fulfilling the philanthropic spirit by helping society through their professional achievements.

4. Common belief has it that physicians are among a community's wealthiest citizens. However, the average debt incurred by a young medical school graduate is more than $100,000. Add to this the indebtedness incurred to set up a practice, and a physician may not feel in the giving mood. For this same reason, physicians may not develop a habit of giving to any charitable cause throughout their lives.

Probably more so than with any other group of people, fund raisers need to keep in mind the axiom of meeting the donor's wishes. When soliciting physicians and attorneys, development professionals need to pay particular attention to the proper cultivation of these prospects. Rather than rushing in with a proposal, take the time to learn about the prospect's interests and wishes. Involve the prospect in the life of the institution before asking for a contribution.[8]

Some of the most generous philanthropists in history have been physicians and attorneys. Whole medical schools, law schools, hospitals, law libraries, and medical laboratories have been galvanized because of the generosity of physicians and attorneys. At any rate, truth in the statement that "physicians and attorneys don't give" is worth exploring further.

Dispelling the myth that doctors don't give is the $10 million campaign for Penn State's Milton S. Hershey Medical Center completed in 1992. During this campaign, more than 92 percent of the medical center's faculty made gifts and pledges. The key to successfully securing major gifts from physicians is no different from any other major gift prospect. The development officer must first focus in on the potential donor's interests. As James Brucker, director of development at Penn State's Hershey Medical Center, points out: "We've found that if you treat physicians the way you would any other major gift prospect, they will respond positively."[9]

Too often, because it is assumed physicians have exorbitant sums of disposable income, they are asked to support everything from Little League to the local opera. Physicians are people too. Penn State's development staff at Hershey put together a sophisticated volunteer structure comprised of physicians who asked their peers to support medical-related programs with resounding success. Development officers ask business people to support the business school and engineers to support engineering programs—why should physicians be treated any differently?

Prospect Management

One of the most important aspects of a major capital campaign is prospect management and the evaluation and rating of major gift prospects. Because most campaigns still validate the tried and tested formula that 90 percent of the gifts come from 10 percent of the donors, it is absolutely vital that a capital campaign secure major commitments very early in the campaign process. Generally speaking, a campaign is doomed to failure if early major commitments are not forthcoming. This is true whether the goal is $1 million or $100 million.

The Prospect Management System

A successful major gifts effort must include the implementation of a prospect management system. The purpose of this system is to guide and direct activity with major gift prospects, using volunteer involvement, senior officers of the institution, and development personnel. Colleges and universities of any size should implement a prospect management system for their ongoing development program, but it is especially vital during a capital campaign. When fully implemented, the prospect management system will regulate all major gift activity for the institution and will be standard operating procedure for major gift fund raising. Kent E. Dove says that:

> The prospect management and tracking system helps an organization manage its involvement with major prospects. Once someone is identified as a prospect, it is imperative that the institution involve that person in its life. Involvement precedes and often begets investment. And investment is the end game in the capital campaign.[10]

The following are the basic elements of a prospect management system, whether the system is a sophisticated, computer-driven model or a more intuitive system that is driven manually:

1. All prospects being pursued for solicitation at the level of $10,000 and above should be assigned to an appropriate development staff member through the prospect management system. That staff member, often in conjunction with a senior administrator, should be charged with the responsibility of escorting his or her prospects through the system.
2. Weekly or monthly prospect management meetings should be held to discuss additions and/or deletions of prospects to the system. Those prospects assigned to a university official who is not a part of the development operation also should be assigned to an individual who does attend the prospect management meetings on a regular basis.
3. Volunteers assigned to a prospect should be so identified by the prospect management system, but should not supplant or interfere with the assignment of a staff member to the case. All prospects should be assigned a staff member.
4. One senior development staff member should have overall responsibility for managing the prospect management system and should be the *only* person authorized to change prospect assignments on a regular basis.
5. Individual staff members assigned to prospects will be identified as the "principal" for those prospects. The principal is responsible for the gift solicitation of that prospect. The principal, in consultation with volunteers and other university or college officials, makes all decisions regarding solicitation, size of the gift request, and the particular appropriate proposal to sug-

gest to the donor. The principal must be held responsible for moving the solicitation process forward at the appropriate time.

6. Requests for assignments and/or deletions of prospects on the prospect management system should be handled routinely at prospect management meetings. All development personnel who call assigned prospects should attend the regular prospect management meetings.

7. A summary of all additions and/or deletions of prospects should be circulated to development personnel on a regular basis.

8. A permanent record of all current assignments on the prospect management system should be available for immediate review by development personnel. In a more sophisticated program, the information should be available for on-line, inquiry on the computer database.

9. Every active prospect appearing on the prospect management system should be assigned a principal.

10. Many times, especially in large universities, other staff members will have identifiable relationships with a prospect. For instance, the development officer in the college of the liberal arts and his or her counterpart in the library might have competing interests in the same prospect. A prospect management system should allow for these competing interests by designating a "secondary assignment" confirming an additional link with the prospect. This second position affirms another interest in the prospect by an additional academic unit and keeps that interest active and before all development staff.

The principal assigned to a prospect has wide-ranging responsibilities for moving the prospect forward for eventual solicitation. These responsibilities must include deciding all "next steps" in cultivating and soliciting a prospect. Every prospect should have a next step. It may be as simple as a target date when the principal will initially contact the prospect, or it may pinpoint subsequent visitation of the prospect, the date when a letter should be sent to that prospect, or a date when the president of the institution should be involved with the prospect.

Generally speaking, each new prospect assigned to a principal should be seen within a reasonable period of time. Prospects who are not visited initially by the principal assigned to them should be reassigned to others.

11. Every prospect in the system should be visited by the staff principal at least once every six months. If a prospect is not important enough to be visited at least every six months, then that prospect may not have bona fide gift potential and thus does not belong on the prospect management system.

12. A principal may wish to employ a team approach to a prospect and include multiple staff members and/or volunteers. The team approach should be encouraged, depending upon the prospect.

13. In consultation with other senior development officials, the principal assigned to a prospect should be responsible for defining the status and rating of that prospect. The principal should make the final decision on the appropriate size of the gift request.

14. Prospects should never be visited or solicited without the permission and advance notice of the principal assigned to the prospect. This will eliminate duplicate solicitation and the multiple visitation of prospects by competing college or university personnel.

Evaluation and Rating of Prospects

Development officers are constantly fretting over the size of the ask for a particular prospect. They obviously want to ask for the maximum gift possible, one that would require a prospect to "stretch" his or her giving. As mentioned previously, major lead gifts are critical to any capital campaign, and benefactors must be challenged in their giving if multimillion dollar goals are to be met.

An old adage in the development business states: "You can never ask for too much." That adage is tired and worn and should be discarded. Benefactors can, indeed, be insulted, confused, and upset by major asks that are far out of proportion to their ability to give. Benefactors can be embarrassed if the campaign ask is out of their league and they simply do not have the resources to come forward at the level that is expected of them.

This is not to say that benefactors should be made to feel "comfortable" about their giving. One multimillion dollar donor was heard to comment after contributing $10 million to his alma mater that one should judge a person "not by how much they give to their alma mater, but by how much they have left!"

Very few benefactors will ever give away their last penny, but it is a development officer's challenge to encourage a benefactor to stretch his or her giving and make a contribution that does not merely reflect excess income but instead demonstrates the prospect's commitment to the institution. In short, a gift should be affordable but perhaps somewhat financially "painful." How does one achieve this delicate balance? The following methods are used frequently to determine the size of a gift request.

Professional Prospect Research. Many colleges and universities with sophisticated development programs have large research staffs that pore over multiple reports, proxy statements, Dun and Bradstreet reports, financial data, and other information to determine the wealth of particular prospects. Regardless of the size of the development operation, a research component should be established during a capital campaign. Even the two- to four-member shop would be wise to implement a research component in its operation. As Bobbie S. Strand says: "The goal of [prospect research] is to support the evaluation of individuals or organizations as prospective donors and to aid in the development of cultivation and solicitation strategies."[11]

Researching prospective donors involves gathering, organizing, and synthesizing information that is then analyzed, screened, and presented in a clear and concise format. In addition, identification of new prospects is a continuing responsibility of this office, which uses a number of resources and techniques to accomplish these ends. High-quality research reports depend upon a team-oriented, well-trained staff working with other development personnel. Because research offices rely extensively on their alumni development databases and on their hard-copy files to provide information on a prospect's past ties and contacts with the institution and his or her giving to the university, proper maintenance of both is of utmost importance to research offices. Research initiates changes in the database as new information surfaces in the course of the development staff's work. Hard-copy files hold correspondence, research reports, reports of contact by development officers, news clippings, past proposals, and gift guidelines. The importance of good, solid reports of contact by development personnel cannot be overemphasized. After every visit to a potential benefactor, a development officer should write a briefing giving firsthand observations, information that may not be available elsewhere.

Development research offices maintain a library of reference materials and various tracking notebooks to follow donor philanthropic activity, research contracts with corporations, faculty proposals to corporations or foundations, and other pertinent information. Research offices also have access to university and public libraries and work closely with librarians to solve research problems. Newspaper libraries vary in their policy of providing information or references to articles over the telephone, but can be important sources of information on articles appearing in newspapers that have not yet been indexed.

County tax offices also vary in their policies of providing information over the telephone. While tax assessments on pieces of property are matters of public record, some tax offices require requests in writing. On occasion, wills can be helpful to the researcher and are on file at most county courthouses. The greatest boon to prospect research has been access to various files through commercial databases. Many sophisticated research offices subscribe to a number of commercial databases. Stock held by company insiders and any holdings they have that constitute 5 percent holdings in public companies are public information and are available from online commercial databases. Indices referencing biographical information are also available. Newspaper and magazine articles on prospects can be retrieved through a simple database search.

Generally, in a sophisticated research office, reports are formatted to include only information helpful to the cultivation effort. In larger research offices, reports are typed by clerical staff, proofed by the researcher, and then read by the research manager before being sent to the appropriate development officer for use in the gift solicitation. The reports are archived on the system and retrieved for updating. All reports should be treated with the highest degree of confidentiality and should not contain any offensive material. According to Strand:

> One of the major problems in major donor research is that most files contain too much of the wrong kind of information and too

few vital data. Quality of information, rather than quantity, should always be the emphasis. Prospect research should deal with these issues:

1. What is this prospect's financial giving capacity?
2. How interested in this institution, or similar institutions, is the prospect?
3. What particular project important to the institution is the prospect most likely to care about?
4. Who can influence the prospect to give to this institution for this purpose at this time?[12]

Volunteer Information. Perhaps the best and most reliable way to determine the size of a gift request is by discussing a particular prospect with an informed volunteer. Often, the volunteer can provide sensitive and confidential information about a particular prospect and the ability of that prospect to make a major commitment to a college or university.

Electronic Screening. Several private companies have electronic-screening tools available and many of these have been customized for fund raising. Electronic screening has become very popular in the development business. Many electronic-screening services maintain databases of geodemographic data supplemented by other indications of wealth, including holding insider stock in public companies. These companies receive a magnetic tape from an institution that then seeks a match with those in its database. If a potential benefactor lives in a city block that is considered to be "upscale," that prospect will be pulled up on the database. One would draw the conclusion that because the individual lives in an affluent, high-rent district, he or she would be capable of making a philanthropic gift to his or her alma mater. Obviously, electronic screening is only one method of determining major gift prospects. Any electronic-screening data should be rigorously reviewed and tested for accuracy.

Periodicals. Research offices scan periodicals for announcements of gifts to other institutions. Most sophisticated research offices subscribe to a variety of periodicals in an attempt to locate prospect information.

Group Screening. Group screening is a traditional prospect evaluation and rating system that is used by a number of colleges and universities. The traditional group screening involves several volunteers reviewing a list that is provided in advance by the development staff. The list is not usually an entire alumni listing, but rather has been refined to a particular universe of prospects. These group screenings can be open discussions or silent screenings. Depending upon the number of prospects to be reviewed and the anticipated giving level, various methodologies can be used. For example, when reviewing a relatively small group of high potential prospects, an initial silent screening by the group, followed by an open discussion, can be very useful. Many times during the silent part of the screening, an individual will rate a prospect much higher or much lower than the rest of the group. Often, whoever rated the prospect out of line from the rest of the group may have some special information about that potential benefactor.

A new twist now exists in group screening. A prospect's name is given to the group and the group is asked about the size of gift that this prospect may make to the university. The volunteers "punch in" their responses on a keyboard, and the data are immediately displayed on a screen for all to see. By using this methodology, the raters have immediate statistical information and can spot any abnormality such as very high or very low ratings. Each rating can be attributed back to a specific volunteer in the room.

A relatively small number of institutions have become more formal in group ratings and have created national programs to conduct group sessions throughout the country. Stanford University, Washington University, and the College of William and Mary are three institutions that have experimented with group rating programs with some success.

Recently Penn State launched its Leadership Evaluation and Assessment Program (LEAP) in an attempt to identify a new wave of major gift prospects throughout the United States. LEAP meetings are being conducted in 50 cities with large concentrations of Penn State alumni. During these sessions, specially selected alumni are asked to screen lists of potential major benefactors and rate what their giving capacity might be in another campaign. These lists are then put into a database and manipulated along with data from other screening sessions. The result is a source of information based on personal knowledge of alumni who work and reside in the same geographic area as the new prospects that have been rated. Through the LEAP project, Penn State hopes to identify as many as 25,000 new potential benefactors at the $10,000 level and above. All of this is being done in anticipation of a second capital campaign.

The Process of Asking for a Gift

Volunteer leaders are the key to success in any major capital campaign. While professional staff are important to the campaign effort, they are no substitute for peers soliciting peers. Success in getting big gifts often has as much to do with the volunteers' influence as the organizational quality or characteristics of any particular program or cause.

A successful gift campaign has a number of requirements, among them: the right volunteer leadership, an effective organizational structure, specific goals and objectives for each campaign committee, a compelling case for support, a favorable economic environment, and strong staff support.

Several factors in the campaign process are cited as most crucial in determining a successful effort.[13]

The Importance of Major Gifts. Ninety percent of the dollars contributed to any program with a major gift focus is raised from fewer than 10 percent of the donors.[14] The importance of major gifts cannot be overemphasized. Those commitments must be made early on for the campaign to be truly successful.

People Give to People. A compelling case for financial support is important, but people do indeed give to people. Major donors are more likely to give at higher levels when they are invited to do so by their peers. Although staff members are very important in moving the solicitation process forward, many times only a peer can convince a particular donor to give in a very significant manner.

Sequential Giving. The largest gifts should be solicited first. Success at this level sets the pace for those with smaller giving capabilities and unquestionably establishes the level of giving for the rest of the campaign. Because the number of any institution's major prospects is limited, great effort must be expended to persuade these initial major prospects to give in proportion to their capacity before any broader-based efforts can begin. Every campaign should move sequentially, allowing the successful solicitation of the largest gift to influence the level of the next-largest gift, and so on. The successful achievement of any campaign is often dictated by how well this early stage of solicitation proceeds. W.R. Brossman states that:

> A $10 thousand project of the women's auxiliary to improve campus landscaping needs a big gift approach just as much as does a multimillion dollar campaign for Harvard. And the same goes for fund raising for athletics, for cooperative efforts such as state association groups of the independent liberal arts colleges, for annual giving programs, for estate planning activities, for memorial projects, and all the rest. Without a nucleus of major gifts, the enterprise will fail.[15]

Formal Solicitations. Major gifts almost never result from letters, phone calls, or casual requests. If a prospect feels that the campaign is not worth more than a letter or a phone call from a volunteer or staff member, he or she is likely to decide that it is not worth the gift. It is absolutely vital, then, that key prospects receive specific written proposals followed by, or in conjunction with, face-to-face meetings. When possible, solicitations should be conducted on a two-on-one basis, as this type of team effort has proven to most effective. Typically the team might include the president or a senior officer of the university, or perhaps selected faculty or a member of the development staff. Generally, the team should include a volunteer leader who is acquainted with the prospect, or another person well known by the prospect. It is almost always a good idea to solicit major gifts in teams. Team members not only reinforce one another but also are better prepared to answer questions and cover any points that may arise during a visit. There are three effective teams.

1. Volunteer and chief executive officer
2. Volunteer and staff member
3. Chief executive officer and staff member

The teams to be used depend on the circumstances. It is hard to rank the combinations by effectiveness, though the first combination often represents the most leverage and the third the least.

The chief executive officer may serve as staff in the first and second combinations and really acts like or fulfills the role of a volunteer, leverage being all-important.[16]

Development personnel should provide cohesive, well-written proposals, tailored to the prospect, for presentation during these visits.

Cultivation: A Process. Major gifts frequently require months or even years of cultivation before being realized. In fact, John Glier, of Grenzebach Glier and Associates, says the average gift of $100,000 or more requires a cultivation period of 18 to 36 months.

Campaign leaders are in a position to conduct informal cultivation activities by entertaining at their homes, hosting small luncheons, or talking with likely prospects on the golf course. Such participation by volunteers in these endeavors is crucial to the success of a campaign.

Cultivation is part of the early leadership phase of the capital campaign, although a volunteer's first visit to a prospective donor probably will not be a solicitation call. Most major gifts are made by individuals who are significantly aware and vitally involved in the activities of the college or university. Cultivation is the process that brings prospects closer to the institution.

Avoid Preemptive Gifts. Allowing prospects to establish their own gift levels without the benefit of focused cultivation and formal solicitation almost always produces gifts that most campaign leaders view as less-than-total commitment. To ensure the success of the capital campaign, solicitation teams must be able to propose the right program opportunity at the right level of giving for each campaign prospect. A campaign must try to avoid allowing a donor to make a gift and/or pledge before the actual proposal is formally made.

Volunteer Giving. A volunteer's confidence in the validity and urgency of the campaign will be a major factor in persuading others to make a significant gift. The best evidence of this confidence is a volunteer's own generous participation at the highest possible level.

Know the Prospect. Volunteers should work with the development staff to know as much as possible about a prospect before the visit.

In all cases, a prospect should not be visited by a volunteer until the volunteer has enough background to ask for the right gift for the most appropriate program. Volunteers should look for ways in which the prospect's investment can allow for greater participation in the program or in the institution as a whole.

Know the Needs. A volunteer must be ready to answer questions about both the institution and the campaign needs. Volunteers should not be expected to know every minor detail about the needs in every division of the college or university. However, a general understanding of the main goals of the campaign and what the funds will be used for is extremely important when soliciting a prospect.

Personal Solicitation—A Key. Major gifts require personal contact. Phone conversations should only be used to discuss the campaign in general terms. A volunteer should find a time and place when the prospect can give full attention to the presentation about the campaign.

Solicit the Best Prospects First. This will give volunteers more confidence for calling on other prospects.

Make the Case. The volunteer should first explain the campaign goals and explore areas of interest. The volunteer should talk about why the institution is worth the prospect's time and resources. Discussion allows a prospect to develop enthusiasm and talk about personal interests and inclinations. First and foremost, a volunteer should be enthusiastic about his or her own interest and commitment in the campaign.

Ask for the Gift. Volunteers should encourage the prospect to make a "stretch" commitment, and should show the prospect the table of required gifts for campaign success. A volunteer should discuss designated gifts, pointing out memorial or tribute opportunities to (subtly) indicate the level of gift the institution is hoping to receive from the prospect. It is not unusual for a volunteer to tell the prospect at this point how much he or she is planning to give to the campaign. This is particularly helpful when the level of gift support from the volunteer matches or exceeds what is being asked of the prospect.

In a face-to-face meeting, perhaps the most difficult part of the solicitation is looking the individual in the eye and asking for an actual amount. It is also the most crucial. From the moment a volunteer and staff member make the call, the prospect is waiting to hear the dollar amount that will be requested. Asking for the gift is the key element of the solicitation. It cannot be left hanging in some vague, misunderstood format. The amount must be stated clearly and definitively, and the prospect must realize that a solicitation for a specific dollar amount has taken place.

Knowing the right way to ask for a gift is something that only will come with practice and experience. The most seasoned development officers who have asked for a gift, literally hundreds of times, can still have difficulty when it comes to requesting a dollar amount. A volunteer—or for that matter, a staff member—should not feel inadequate simply because he or she finds this extremely important part of the solicitation difficult. The bottom line is that it is difficult, but essential.

The gift amount should always be decided upon in advance and supported with a specific written proposal provided by the staff. Prospects will appreciate being asked to consider a targeted program or programs, and a specific dollar amount. The proposal should be tailored to a prospect's personal interests and needs as best as these qualities are known at the time.

A volunteer and staff member should always keep the discussion focused and seek resolution. Initially negative responses are common, and a volunteer should not back away from the solicitation if the prospect does not respond positively.

Generally speaking, a lower gift should be negotiated only when the target asked is clearly beyond the reach of a particular prospect. Development officers have numerous stories of prospects who have rejected initial proposals only to make much larger gifts after a lengthy period of cultivation.

Explore Ways to Give. Volunteers should remind the prospect that gifts can be made with a variety of assets, including stocks, securities, real estate, insurance, and bequests, as well as cash. If an outright gift is not possible, volunteers should suggest the deferred gift and remember to emphasize tax advantages, even if tax incentives do not seem to be the primary motivation for making a contribution.

Use Recognition Strategy. Gift naming opportunities provide an important impetus, particularly at major gift levels.

Seek Pledges. Volunteers should encourage donors to give the most generous gift possible by extending payments over a period of years.

Volunteers should not be reluctant to leave pledge forms in the hands of prospects who do not make a commitment and sign the pledge immediately. It is important to keep in mind that when asked for a major commitment, the prospect will probably need time to consider the proposal and will not make a split-second decision. Even though some professionals may argue against it, one should allow prospects to take pledge forms and proposals home, discuss the proposal with family members, and think about the proposed gift's affect on the institution. Big gifts to colleges and universities are generally made only after much deliberation and thought, and it is wise to allow the prospect to have enough time for proper reflection.

A gift pledge commitment should be made in writing using the official pledge commitment form. This is required so that the gift can be officially counted toward the campaign goal and be recognized by campaign leadership. Prospects also recognize that the pledge is a serious investment in the institution and understand the need for adequate documentation.

Don't Push. Major gifts cannot be hurried. As gifts get larger, the time required to reach a decision is generally longer. The prospect may want to consult with his or her family or personal staff and possibly a financial or legal advisor before deciding upon the size and method of giving. It is important to always encourage such consultation.

This is not to suggest that a development officer or volunteer should not continue to follow up with the prospect in a meaningful way; perhaps set a date in the future to discuss the pledge. But it is crucial to be sensitive to the prospect and allow adequate time for a genuinely reflective decision.

Be Positive. Volunteers should not become discouraged. The job may be a difficult one, but the benefits to the institution are immense. Nothing is more important to the institution than the campaign. Development officers must remember that they are helping to change the institution for the better: they are positioning it for the future.

Leave a Proposal. The written proposal seems to be a stumbling block for many development officers. Many development directors have failed because of their inability to put the gift request down in writing. For some reason, the campaign proposal lends itself to procrastination and, many times, is the last item that is "pulled together" prior to the solicitation. Development officers will barter, beg, and plead so that "they" don't have to write the proposal.

Proposal writing for prospects should be neither complex nor difficult. The proposal is simply a statement in writing of the most critical reasons why the campaign must be successful. A shorter proposal, rather than longer, is preferable, and the author advises a proposal that is no longer than two pages. This should be adequate space to delineate the needs of the campaign and the specific gift proposal and amount for the individual prospect. Both of the $10 million gifts received in The Campaign for Penn State came about from a formal, personal solicitation with a delivered proposal of no more than two pages. One's words in a proposal do not need to be eternal to be immortal. Besides, benefactors do not want to take time to read lengthy proposals that go on interminably with lofty language but relatively little substance.

Proposals should always state an amount and a pledge term so that benefactors are clearly aware of the expectation of the institution. Some experts will claim that stating this amount early in the proposal is better, although anecdotal evidence suggests that this is not necessarily an important factor provided that the gift ask amount is clearly visible in the letter, preferably within the two-page format.

Many development officers will ask what kind of format will get a better reception, a proposal format or letter format. The letter format is a much warmer communication to the prospect. Proposals seem much too clinical and technical for individual benefactors.

It should be pointed out that many corporate foundations, and foundations in general, will require formal proposals of considerable length. Each foundation is generally different, and their guidelines should be consulted prior to proposal writing. However, for individual benefactors a two-page letter format is recommended.

Common Mistakes in Major Gift Solicitations

Thinking That Someone Else Will Raise the Major Gifts. Big gifts don't just happen; they require considerable preparation by staff and volunteers. One volunteer can't think that another will take care of the big gifts. It is the responsibility of the development professional or volunteer to find gift support for the institution. It is imperative to think creatively and positively.

Not Understanding That the Best Major Gift Prospects Are Past Donors. In any size campaign past contributors are the best source for future support. Don't make the mistake of thinking that a person who has given generously has exhausted all of his or her assets. Generally speaking, wealthy people regenerate wealth and are constantly adding to their portfolio and building capital. Don't allow a wealthy, generous benefactor to feel left out simply because he or she hasn't been "asked enough." These individuals are the campaign's best prospects, and, generally speaking, they should be asked first in any major campaign.

Not Asking for a Gift. This omission is the bane of all fund raising. The president accompanies a volunteer to ask for a major commitment from a prospect, but somehow the proposal is not quite put on the table. Either the president is or the volunteer is shy or a combination of both. Not asking for the gift will absolutely destroy a campaign. Nothing can hinder a campaign more than failure to ask. No magic is required—just a strong will, intestinal fortitude, and the ability to look a person in the eye and ask. Just ask.

Not Asking for a Large Enough Gift. Generally speaking, donors are not forthcoming with major commitments unless they are asked. Million-dollar gifts flow to an institution only after a staff member or volunteer has specifically requested that support. Don't expect the large gifts to walk in the door without cultivation and a precise, detailed presentation.

Failing to Cultivate the Prospect Adequately Before Solicitation.
Major gifts take time—more than first anticipated. A volunteer and
staff member should not be too quick to place a proposal before a
prospect. Be certain that the prospect is ready to receive it. Generally speaking, when a prospect is not ready, he or she will not make
a gift or will make a much smaller gift than that requested.

**Not Knowing Enough About the Prospect's Personal and Program
Interests.** Prospects make major gifts to areas where they have a
personal and programmatic interest. An individual who, for example, is closely aligned with liberal arts should be encouraged to
give to liberal arts. If a prospect never had any interest in another
program and shows no inclination to give to anything other than
liberal arts, why try to switch his or her loyalty? Ask donors to give
where they are most comfortable giving and don't try to change
their allegiances to other projects that do not hold special interest.

Not Fully Understanding the Case for Support. Volunteers must
understand why they are seeking major gift support. Prospects
readily gauge the interest of a volunteer and can tell during the
solicitation if that volunteer is committed to the program. A
noncommitted, uninterested volunteer only hinders the solicitation effort. Volunteers must be wedded to the case for support,
and must understand the needs of the institution and why the institution is seeking philanthropic support.

**Not Being Fully Prepared with Alternatives for a Particular Pros-
pect.** Even though staff members have done a magnificent job trying to determine the interest areas of a prospect and have spent
many hours putting together the proper gift solicitation, it may
still be unappealing to a particular benefactor. Volunteers and staff
must be ready to suggest support of alternative projects and programs to a potential benefactor and must be able to talk creatively
during the solicitation. Don't be caught off guard when a potential benefactor says, "I am not really interested in that project. What
else do you have to offer?"

Failing to Talk About the Benefits of Giving. Many benefits will
accrue to an individual who decides to make a commitment to his
or her college or university. A volunteer should be prepared to
talk about both the tangible and the intangible benefits.

Failing to Involve the Right People in the Solicitation. Staff members should match volunteers with prospects. This should not be a simple method of pairing off geographic volunteers with prospects in their region. For major gift prospects, much discussion should take place as to who should be the appropriate person to make the presentation.

A particular case involved a major presentation by the president of the university, soliciting a Pittsburgh-based foundation for $500,000 for an academic program in one of Penn State's colleges. As it turned out, the entire solicitation was spent talking about Penn State football and Joe Paterno. Two weeks later, Penn State received a $1 million gift for the Paterno Libraries Endowment. It might be said this approach used the wrong volunteer—but with gratifying results.

Relying Too Heavily on Development Staff to Provide the Initiative. Staff members are critical to the success of the campaign. Their importance cannot be overstated. They will help to lead and guide the effort and serve as the catalyst to make the campaign happen.

However, relying too heavily on development staff also can lead a campaign to failure. Staff are important, but volunteers are more important when soliciting major gifts. Volunteers must not rely on staff to tell them everything to do. Volunteers must be active in their own right and should not wait for the campaign staff to locate sources of support. On the other hand, volunteers should not pursue their own agenda without staff input. Certainly their activities must be coordinated by the development personnel. Volunteers should be encouraged to think creatively and cannot expect that their every movement will be orchestrated by development personnel.

Notes

1. Jon Van Til and Associates, *Critical Issues in American Philanthropy: Strengthening Theory and Practice.* (San Francisco: Jossey-Bass Inc., 1990), p. 9.
2. Barbara Brittingham, T. Pezzullo, "The Campus Green: Fund Raising in Higher Education," in *ASHE-ERIC Higher Education Report Number 1.* (Washington, DC: School of Education and Human Development, The George Washington University, 1990), p. 40.
3. G. David Gearhart, "A Study of the Relationship Between the Preparation for and Initiation of a Capital Fund-Raising Campaign in a Major Research University and Two Types of Organizational Structure." p. 173, Ed.D. diss., University of Arkansas, Fayetteville, Arkansas. 1989.
4. Kent E. Dove, *Conducting a Successful Capital Campaign: A Comprehensive Guide for Nonprofit Organizations.* (San Francisco: Jossey-Bass Inc., 1988), p. 43.
5. Jerold Panas, *Megagifts: Who Gives Them, Who Gets Them.* (Chicago: Pluribus Press, 1984), p. 35.
6. Harold J. Seymour, *Designs for Fund-Raising: Principles, Patterns, Techniques.* (New York: McGraw Hill, 1966), p. 6.
7. Richard Kirkland Jr., "Should You Leave It All to the Children?" in *Fortune vol. 114*: (September 29, 1986): 18–26.
8. Holly Hall, "Getting Doctors to Give," in *The Chronicle of Philanthropy vol. iii no. 11*: (March 26, 1991): 18–21.
9. Doug Stanfield, "Doctors Don't Give," in *Fund Raising Management*: (April 1993): 23–27, 44.
10. Dove, *Conducting a Successful Capital Campaign: A Comprehensive Guide for Nonprofit Organizations*, p. 114.
11. Bobbie J. Strand, "Building a Donor Information Base," in A. W. Rowland, ed., *Handbook of Institutional Advancement: A Modern Guide to Effective Management, Institutional Relations, Fund-Raising, Alumni Administration, Government Relations, Publications, Periodicals, and Enrollment Management* (San Francisco: Jossey-Bass Inc., 1986), p. 337.
12. Strand, "Building a Donor Information Base," in *Handbook of Institutional Advancement: A Modern Guide to Effective Management, Institutional Relations, Fund-Raising, Alumni Administration,*

Government Relations, Publications, Periodicals, and Enrollment Management, pp. 339–340.

13. *The Campaign for Penn State: Guide for Volunteers.* (University Park, Pennsylvania: The Pennsylvania State University, 1987), p. 1. [Brochure].

14. Dove, *Conducting a Successful Capital Campaign: A Comprehensive Guide for Nonprofit Organizations,* p. 67.

15. W. R. Brossman, "The Central Importance of Large Gifts," in Francis C. Pray, ed., *Handbook for Educational Fund Raising: A Guide to Successful Principles and Practices for Colleges, Universities, and Schools* (San Francisco: Jossey-Bass Inc., 1981), p. 70.

16. Thomas E. Broce, *Fund Raising: The Guide to Raising Money from Private Sources 2nd ed.* (Norman, OK: University of Oklahoma Press, 1979), p. 226.

S I X

Campaign Particulars

The Six Phases

It is helpful to look at a capital campaign as a series of phases. These phases often overlap, and sometimes it is difficult to determine when one phase has been completed and another one has begun. The phases are interconnecting and interwoven. It is possible, however, to define each phase in general terms.

Six phases in a capital campaign can be identified.

1. **Quiet Planning Phase.** Depending on the breadth and scope of a campaign as well as on its sophistication and complexity, this phase could, in fact, last for several years. Some institutions begin planning a capital campaign two, three, or four years prior to ever soliciting the first gift. The preceding chapters have laid out the various elements necessary in planning a capital campaign, and it may take at least this long to put these elements into place. An institution that has been planning a capital campaign for several years should not be concerned about the tremendous time commitment in the planning process unless the campaign has, in fact, been discussed in a public forum. It is difficult to hold the attention of important volunteers if the planning phase is announced in public. This phase should be internal, involving primarily institutional staff, and should be a confidential preparation outlining the various elements from an internal standpoint. Some institutions

113

begin this phase of a campaign literally weeks or months after just having completed a major capital campaign.

2. **Advance Gift Phase.** During this phase, which may last one to two years, the campaign becomes public to a small group of benefactors and volunteers, while the major campaign committee is recruited, and the lead gifts are solicited. This phase is characterized by major gift activity with the institution's most important and generous benefactors. The success of the advance gift phase often determines the overall success of the campaign.

3. **Public Phase.** This phase is characterized by the public announcement to the news media of the capital campaign and the determination and announcement of the goal. The public phase of the campaign can stretch anywhere from two to four years, depending on the overall length of the capital campaign. Major gift activity will continue throughout this phase, and the garnering of gifts of at least $100,000 and above will be of particular importance during this phase.

   During the public phase, it is likely (and desirable) that media attention will focus on the campaign, and various volunteer donor events are initiated. These events could include a kickoff for the campaign, announcing the goal as well as the amount of funds raised in the advance gift phase. It is during the public phase that the faculty/staff campaign, student campaign, and, perhaps, community campaign could be initiated. This adds public attention to the effort.

4. **Plateau Phase.** At some point during the public phase of the campaign, the campaign will likely enter into a "plateau" phase—a time when volunteers and benefactors tire of the campaign and are ready for its completion. In a five-year campaign, this phase generally occurs three or four years into the campaign. Volunteers are fatigued and ready to get the campaign behind them. Not every campaign experiences a plateau phase, but if it should occur, an institution must find ways to reinvigorate those involved in the effort.

   The establishment of a new (higher) goal and new (longer) timetable can help to breathe new life into the campaign.

5. **Final Phase.** The final phase of the campaign is built around the achievement of the goal and pushing toward successful completion. Goal attainment, in itself, energizes the commit-

tee, and many benefactors who have not already made commitments will come forward in an effort to help put the campaign "over the top." At this time previous benefactors often increase their commitments in hopes of achieving the goal.

During the final phase, donor-recognition events should take place to honor major benefactors for their philanthropy. An institution may be interested in a final campaign event that brings together the various constituencies of the campaign, honoring them and their multiple achievements.

The final phase should be an important time for the institution to assess what the campaign has meant in terms of additional resources for academic programs.

6. **Post-Campaign Phase.** Immediately following the end of the campaign, campaign staff should assess the success of the campaign and create a post-campaign plan to continue philanthropic support. Even though the campaign has concluded, major gift fund raising must remain as an important part of the development program. Hopefully, the institution will have reached a level of gift support that can be sustained, even in the off years of the capital campaign. The capital campaign also should be expected to boost the level of annual giving. The post-campaign phase is a time to sharpen the focus of the development program and to decide where resources can best be applied to continue to attract the highest level of gift support possible.

An example of a campaign timetable characterizing the six components is contained in appendix G.

Percent of Goal in Hand
Prior to Public Announcement

A capital campaign should never be publicly announced without a percentage of the goal already committed.[1]

Some professionals will argue that at least 50 percent of goal should be committed prior to public announcement. For capital campaigns above $100 million, the achievement of 50 percent may not be possible. A more practical aim is to achieve at least one-third of the goal in pledges and commitments prior to announcing the capital campaign publicly. One-third of the goal in hand is a respectable figure that shows forward momentum as well as the ability of the college or university to attract major commitments. Having attracted $5 million in a $15 million capital campaign or $100 million in a $300 million capital campaign is a notable achievement and will be viewed by the public as substantial progress toward the goal.

While some may argue that the larger the amount in hand prior to public announcement the better, this can send a signal to the public that the achievement of the goal is too easy or too simple and that the goal has not been set high enough. This may, in fact, cause donors to lower their sights in terms of their own campaign giving. It is never wise to give benefactors and volunteers the feeling that the achievement of the goal will not require a stretch commitment on their part. Do not make the process look too easy.

Cost/Budget of the Capital Campaign

The worn out phrase, "You have to spend money to make money," can certainly be applied in the context of a capital campaign. Capital campaigns are doomed to failure when senior administrators fail to recognize that the campaign will, in fact, cost money. It is simply not possible to run the effort without an infusion of resources over and above the normal operating budget of a development office.

Studies have revealed that the cost to raise a dollar can range widely from a low of 5 cents to a high of 90 cents.

As Margaret Duronio and B.A. Loessin state: "It is difficult to compare fund-raising costs and budgets across institutions."[2] The average for *all* philanthropic organizations, not just colleges and universities, is about 20 percent. Jon Van Til and Associates point out that "the Council of Better Business Bureaus (CBBB) states that fund-raising expenses that exceed 35 percent are excessive."[3]

The author knows of no definitive studies that earmark capital campaign fund-raising costs at a particular percentage. For some time, principals at Grenzebach Glier and Associates have maintained that fund-raising costs in a capital campaign should be approximately 10 percent of the funds raised. Therefore, if a campaign is raising $100 million, it will probably cost in the neighborhood of $10 million to raise those funds. This figure seems to have some credibility. In fact, the American Association of Fund Raising Counsels (AAFRC) recommends that capital campaign costs stay between 5 and 10 cents per dollar raised.[4]

Perhaps a better way to look at fund-raising costs for a capital campaign is to review a list of those items that will require an extraordinary appropriation of funds. The following is a partial list:

1. **Travel Budgets.** Expect as much as a 50 percent increase during the first three years of the campaign.
2. **Staff Costs.** Staffing costs inevitably increase, and an institution should be ready to add staff in a number of key areas.
3. **Donor Relations Costs.** Donor relations and donor-recognition costs climb markedly, particularly during the final stages of the campaign.
4. **Publications Costs.** Campaign publications, including the campaign brochure and periodic public reports, require additional resources for the development office.
5. **Volunteer Cultivation Costs.** The institution must appropriate additional funds for the cultivation of volunteers. Numerous volunteer meetings must take place throughout the life of the campaign.
6. **Administrative Services Costs.** An institution may need to upgrade its records system in anticipation of a capital campaign, and this will require additional resources.
7. **Video Costs.** An institution may want to create a campaign video; production costs can be extremely expensive.
8. **Costs for Kickoff and Concluding Events.** A campaign kickoff event and a campaign conclusion are not only time-consuming from a staff standpoint, but also quite costly. An institution should appropriate funds as needed for these two important events.
9. **Professional Fees.** Depending on the expertise of the existing staff, there may be an increase in planned gifts to the institution during the capital campaign. Attorneys' fees and other funds for expert advice in planned giving might be required. If campaign counsel is employed, these costs must be factored in.

Information Systems

When "gearing up" for a campaign, one of the frequently overlooked areas is the information system. It is one of the most important aspects to the success of a major fund-raising effort, not to mention ongoing development operation. Conversely, in the absence of a fully functional system that is in tune with the needs of the staff, the efforts made toward dollar goals and the cultivation of prospects can be quickly erased. Mistakes seems to compound themselves and what was a simple problem one day becomes a catastrophe the next, drawing development officers away from the central purpose of raising money: A $1,000 gift is acknowledged as $100; the bio field will not accommodate a last name with more than 10 letters; there is not a clear list of everyone who gave $1,000 and up last year and live in a defined geographic region; and on and on. This leads staff members to distrust the information that is in the system and to attempt to find other ways to meet information needs. Mini-info systems are built by area, department, or in some cases, by individual. Again, time is taken away from the purpose at hand. The problem continues to compound itself.

A successful fund-raising operation cannot operate without a user-friendly, flexible, reliable, management information system. With that in mind, three critical aspects of a good system should be reviewed: application software, data management, and resources.

Many software programs are literally homegrown and built over years, adding new fields when needed. However, today's market offers a variety of sophisticated alumni development programs that meet the needs of all types of institutions. They are user-friendly, efficient, and provide room for growth.

Most systems come as a package, with elements that an institution pays for but does not necessarily need, or enhancements that are not available with the package and cost extra. Nor are these systems inexpensive. When considering the cost of building a personal system, it is at least worth the time to investigate the possibilities.

Application software programs typically address four areas of information: biographical, gifts, pledges, and memberships.

Biographical information has become much more than name and address. Today's fund raisers and alumni professionals need to be aware of family relationships, interests, business information, volunteer activities, preferred mailing address, preferred mailing name, nicknames, and so on. The system needs to be capable of generating personalized mail with preferred salutations in a quick, efficient manner. The marketplace has grown accustomed to this kind of product.

Likewise, gift and pledge information is complex, and a system must handle these without mistakes. Gifts that are split between husband and wife, matching gifts, pledge payments, pledge reminder, gift receipts—all have to be integrated into a system and automated as much as possible, but still provide the users with flexibility to meet the individual needs of the institution.

Perhaps the best indicator of a good system is the ease with which information can be entered and retrieved. The human element is the most critical when measuring the integrity of the database. Therefore, a system that simplifies the process of data entry not only saves time, but reduces the chance of error. A good system will not only provide the flexibility and breadth to track information in many different ways, but also keep the data-entry steps to a minimum.

Although the mark of a good information system is its capacity to store information in a variety of ways, the true test is its capability to provide that information in a usable format. Today's advancement professional requires more information in more ways in less time. The combination of high-speed networks, sophisticated software programs, and advanced technology have reduced turnaround times by significant amounts. Statistical data (counts, lists, or labels) that required two to three days—sometimes even a week—to formulate and retrieve can now be done by "on-line select procedures" in just hours.

Perhaps the most important tools to the fund-raising professional, especially during a campaign, are the reports generated by the system. Accurate, timely reports—daily, weekly, and monthly—provide critical information and play an important role in the decision-making process. The questions then become: What information is needed? In what format? How often? All of these questions need to be thoroughly addressed before entering a campaign and assessing whether the current system has the capabilities required.

Appendix H lists several companies that specialize in providing alumni/development data systems.

The Gift Range Chart

Early in campaign planning, it is important to create what is commonly referred to as "the gift range chart," which is designed to show the number of gifts that are required at certain levels in order to reach the goal. In other words, how many gifts of $1 million will be needed to achieve a goal of $100 million? How many gifts of $500,000 will be required? After determining the number of gifts that the campaign would like to achieve in any one category, it is then important to quantify the number of prospects needed to achieve the number of actual gifts at that level on the gift range chart. If an institution has listed five $1 million gifts as necessary to reach the overall goal, then there will be a corresponding number of prospects that should be contacted for gifts at that level. Appendix I contains gift range charts for campaigns of $10 million and $100 million.

The number of prospects that are needed for the achievement of a gift in a particular category is somewhat subjective. Kent E. Dove states that, "it is a generally accepted rule of thumb that an institution must have at least four legitimate gift prospects for each major gift required."[5] The Campaign for Penn State had a proposal funding rate of approximately 30 percent. This percentage is probably high compared to other institutions, some of which achieve less than a 10 percent proposal funding rate.

Therefore, using the 25 percent success rate as proposed by Dove, one would draw the conclusion that in order to achieve 10 $1 million gifts in a capital campaign, it will be necessary to have a minimum of 40 to 50 viable prospects who have the potential to contribute at this level. This is a somewhat liberal estimate, and this author maintains that an institution would be more likely to require 70 to 100 viable prospects to secure the 10 $1 million gifts referenced above.

A gift range chart should not be created in a vacuum. It should be tied to an institution's prospect management system, and the number of legitimate prospects an institution has will have a significant impact when creating the gift range chart.

Obviously, development officials must "labor in reality" when creating the chart. The author is reminded of a *New Yorker* cartoon where several people were sitting around a table planning a benefit concert. They were trying to determine what the price of the tickets should be in order to achieve $50,000. One participant exclaimed, "I've got a good idea, let's sell one ticket for $50,000!"

If the gift range chart is tied to the prospect management system, development officers may be surprised at how closely gifts will fall along the lines of the gift range chart. A carefully crafted gift range chart helps an institution track its progress toward achievement of the goal.

The Term of the Capital Campaign

The length of a capital campaign normally spans from three to seven years, and it is recommended that no campaign have a length longer than seven years. (Chapter 8 will discuss this further.) The rationale for this is that capital campaigns can sustain neither themselves nor the enthusiasm of volunteers much longer than seven years. Those institutions that launch capital campaigns with a ten-year term or more are probably not actually conducting capital campaigns, but rather labeling their annual ongoing support structure a capital campaign.

Most institutions appear to have a campaign length of five years.[6] Five years is a reasonable period in which to galvanize volunteer support and keep the volunteer enthusiasm from waning. The term of a campaign will depend a great deal on the size and complexity of the institution. Larger, more diverse institutions with multiple constituencies may need to expand the number of years past five in order to complete all of the major gift solicitations required. Institutions with smaller alumni constituencies may be able to complete the major gift process in a much shorter period of time.

Bearing on the length of a capital campaign is, of course, the continuity and longevity of staff and key volunteers. It is important that the president of the institution remain in office throughout the life of the capital campaign. Changing presidents in the middle of a capital campaign can be most destructive to the overall process. Likewise, losing senior development staff can cause an institution to lose momentum in its capital campaign. Stability of staff must remain a priority throughout the life of the campaign.

Similarly, key volunteers must sign on for a definitive length of time, and it is important that the key volunteers not only maintain interest but be officially connected to the campaign throughout its term. The longer a campaign exists, the more difficult the continuity of staff and volunteers will be.

Campaign Cash Flow

A capital campaign does not necessarily create significant changes in the institution's operating cash flow in the short term. Most commitments to a capital campaign are pledged on a multiyear basis. It is difficult to explain to many groups, particularly faculty, that a $100 million capital campaign will not produce $100 million in hand by the final year of the campaign. The institution will receive numerous planned gifts that may pay income to a benefactor, but will have to wait a period of years to receive the actual financial benefits of the gift.

Campaign volunteers and staff should educate internal and external constituents about this issue early on in the campaign.

The Pledge Form

Chapter 8 discusses the importance of the pledge in more detail. The pledge form is an important element in the campaign, and its design should be a campaign priority.

Three types of pledge forms should be designed. The first is a legally binding document and should be used whenever possible (see appendix J).

The second pledge form can be used as a statement of intent by a benefactor and is not necessarily binding on the benefactor or his or her estate. Many donors are reluctant to sign a document that will bind their estate should they not fulfill their pledge during their lifetime (see appendix K).

Finally, officers should create a third pledge form when gifts of cash or securities, rather than planned gifts, are required (see appendix L).

Frequency Between Capital Campaigns

As previously stated, many institutions begin planning for a second capital campaign almost immediately after the first has concluded. It gives a sense, internally, that the institution is constantly in campaign mode. It is important, however, that the quiet and public phases of a campaign be separated by a period of years from a second effort. At least five years should interrupt two major, comprehensive campaigns. The two most important considerations are volunteer and donor fatigue.

Immediately following an intense solicitation effort, it may be difficult to stir up volunteer support. Some "breathing room" will be necessary before launching another effort. Perhaps more important than this, however, is donor fatigue. The institution must give donors the opportunity to "catch up" prior to launching another major effort. Donors will be paying multiple-year campaign pledges, and it is wise to consider the pledge period of major benefactors carefully.

On the other hand, development officials should not wait so long that major prospects and benefactors have developed new and additional loyalties, pledging substantial amounts to competing priorities rather than reconsidering support to the college or university. Wealthy individuals continue the production of wealth and build capital throughout their lives, and it is likely that they will be making major commitments to some other entity. Institutions should not allow major prospects to develop other interests and philanthropies by unnecessarily delaying a second campaign.

Notes

1. Kent E. Dove, *Conducting a Successful Capital Campaign: A Comprehensive Guide for Nonprofit Organizations.* (San Francisco: Jossey-Bass Inc., 1988), p. 147.
2. Margaret A. Duronio, B.A. Loessin, *Effective Fund Raising in Higher Education: Ten Success Stories.* (San Francisco: Jossey-Bass Inc., 1991), p. 5.
3. Jon Van Til and Associates, *Critical Issues in American Philanthropy: Strengthening Theory and Practice.* (San Francisco: Jossey-Bass Inc., 1990), p. 56.
4. James M. Greenfield, "Fund-Raising Costs and Credibility: What the Public Needs to Know," in *NSFRE Journal* (Autumn 1988).
5. Dove, *Conducting a Successful Capital Campaign: A Comprehensive Guide for Nonprofit Organizations,* p. 73.
6. Brakeley, John Price Jones, Inc., "Capital Campaigns 1991–92," in *Capital Campaign Report.* (Stamford, CT: Brakeley John Price Jones, Inc., Spring 1992).

SEVEN

Public Relations for the Campaign

Fund-raising and public relations experts must find ways to collaborate when organizing a public relations plan for a capital campaign. According to Roger L. Williams, a major trend began in the late 1980s. "Public relations and development, once the surly partners of a shotgun marriage, have learned to get along famously. The main reason: the many capital campaigns that colleges and universities have launched."[1]

Williams surveyed 12 colleges and universities that were involved in capital campaigns and discovered that both fund-raising and public relations officials recognized the importance of the public relations function in their campaigns.

The organizational structure of an institution's public relations component will heavily influence the communications plan of a capital campaign. The communications function must be closely aligned with (or report to) the public relations personnel, provided the institutional advancement program is integrated under one senior officer. The development communications arm of the campaign can and should continue to report to the public relations experts under this integrated model. It is important, however, that with any organizational model the public relations and development personnel work in tandem to create the best public relations plan possible for the campaign.

Institutional and Campaign Identity

A strong visual identity system for an institution and its campaign is often overlooked but can be an extremely important public relations initiative.

An institutional and campaign identity helps eliminate confusion in the minds of target audiences, and unifies and strengthens an institution and all its component parts. It projects an image of excellence and cohesiveness that is important in attracting major gift support. Not only will a campaign need a definitive name, but it will also need a "look" and graphic identity that will help to ensure that the institution's many diverse parts have visual consistency. An identity system allows an institution to communicate, at every opportunity, a sense of stature, history, and quality in keeping with its stated commitment to greater levels of excellence. Roger Williams, who masterminded Penn State's identity system before the launch of its comprehensive capital campaign in 1985, describes an identity as:

> [a] comprehensive positioning exercise. . . It involves an organization's basic competencies, its market products, competitive differentiation, and strategic goals. In the sharply competitive climate of the 80s, an identity program can be a superb management tool. It can help to refine or even drive an institution's strategic plan. More mythically, it can serve as a self-fulfilling prophecy.[2]

Robert Topor, when addressing the issue of institutional image, states:

> Your first objective is to create and communicate some positive common image ideas appropriate to all audiences. Another objective is to create and communicate discreet image aspects to discreet target audiences. Think of your institutional image as a central theme with variations on that theme for various audiences. The common aspects are most critical. They will be the ones that position your institution in the marketplace—that is, these aspects will determine the perceived relationship of your institution to its competitors.[3]

A campaign must present a clear, focused, and consistent communications program. It must allow the institution to communicate its cohesiveness and must give the public a sense of direction and leadership.

Williams provides five suggestions for those institutions considering an identity program in anticipation of a capital campaign. These are presented in figure 7.1.

The Campaign Public Relations Plan

Robert L. Krit offers the following on public relations: "Good public relations involves the development and maintenance of good

---

Figure 7.1   Five Suggestions for Developing an Identity Program

1. Select an external firm with expertise to do the research and create the graphic identity system. Do not try to do this through an internal committee or turn it into a student logo contest. Too much is at stake not to have the very best objective expertise at your disposal.
2. Realize that such a program cannot succeed without your president's support.
3. Reconcile yourself to the fact that identity programs take time and energy even at small institutions. As organizational change enthusiasts can well imagine, alterations to an institution's aesthetic symbols do not come easily; everybody from the janitor to the president of the faculty senate brings subjective baggage to the introduction of a new identity. It is a highly visible project, and everyone will have an opinion.
4. Realize, too, that even with top-level administrative support, you still have to "sell" the new identity to the rest of your academic community. An identity program finds greater acceptance in the corporate world, where the CEO manages its adoption, and only those employees seeking new careers challenge its validity. In academe, faculty and staff are not so easily impressed, and they often resist mandates, especially when they don't like what is being mandated. Therefore, much work and persuasion are involved in meeting with individuals and groups to explain how the new identity will better serve their unit's special needs.
5. Finally, tie the identity to the substantive directions in which the institution is moving. Identity is not fluff, puffery, or icing on the cake. It can be an invaluable management tool in finding and communicating the unique essence and aspirations of an institution—in that process attracting resources and support essential to the institution's future.[4]

relations with whatever segment of the public you may wish to reach, including those in need of your services as well as those on whom you must depend for support."[5] An institution should devise a public relations plan as part of its overall campaign planning. The plan should have definite goals and objectives and should lay out a precisely targeted audience. Audiences important to the campaign include alumni and friends of the institution as well as internal constituents—faculty, staff, and students.

The campaign plan should build momentum with precampaign publicity objectives, with the hope of escalating to a crescendo in anticipation of announcing the campaign goal and public phase.

Roger Williams says that public relations can contribute to educational fund raising on three basic levels:

1. Contextual, creating visibility for the institution and enhancing its reputation with a variety of constituencies so that fund raising can succeed
2. Strategic, helping to resolve the what and why issues of educational fund raising
3. Tactical, determining how to fulfill goals and objectives with specific events and activities[6]

The purpose of the campaign public relations plan is to create expectations of success among key constituencies. The plan should be designed to keep the various publics informed about campaign progress and to create a mood of forward movement and success.

A public relations plan can fall into four distinct phases.

Phase I: Precampaign Publicity

Create excitement about the campaign and the upcoming announcement of the goal and objectives. This phase should be delicately handled so as not to abridge the confidentiality of the goal and campaign announcement prematurely. The announcement of the campaign chairperson and the lead campaign committee will be important components of this phase.

Phase II: Announcement of the Campaign

Plan a formal event to announce the goal of the campaign and its various components. Rely on the public relations component of the university to implement the campaign announcement and public phase.

Phase III: Informational Phase

During this phase, publicity centers on announcing major gifts. This will create a sense of momentum and will help to energize the campaign's key constituents.

Care should always be taken to announce gifts of benefactors in the medium that will give maximum visibility to the gift. Special attention should be given to the benefactor's wishes. This may include releasing the information to hometown newspapers, special professional journals, and other outlets that will publicize the gift in the most appropriate way.

Staff, in consultation with volunteers, should decide early on in campaign planning the level of campaign gifts that should be publicized. This will depend a great deal on the level of gifts that are expected in the campaign, but development officers should be sensitive, and only publicize those gifts that will help to serve as a multiplier for other contributions. Publicizing smaller contributions will only set the tone of the campaign at that level and will not help to position the campaign as a major gift effort. A potential benefactor who reads about a gift from an individual who had the capability of making a much larger contribution may be apt to reduce his or her pledge accordingly. At Penn State, gift publicity is generally not offered below the $50,000 level. Naturally, flexibility must be maintained as there certainly are some situations where gifts below $50,000 may require publicity. But generally speaking, announcing major commitments early in the campaign will help to set the level of support to achieve the goal.

Phase IV: Concluding Campaign and Post-Campaign Phase

Building toward the successful conclusion of the campaign and attainment of the goal in the immediate post-campaign environment is the last phase of the campaign public relations plan. This phase focuses on the success of the campaign and points to the achievements of the effort toward strengthening academic programs. An institution's constituency is interested in what happens immediately following the successful conclusion of the campaign, and a carefully structured public information plan to inform volunteers and other constituents is essential.

Internal University Publications

Keep the internal institutional community apprised of campaign planning and direction. Often, faculty and staff who are not directly related to the campaign can lose track of the campaign's progress without a carefully structured informational network. Use internal university publications, such as the student newspaper, an administrative informational newspaper, and a presidential letter to faculty and staff, to keep internal constituencies "wired in" throughout the life of the campaign. Even though these venues will not necessarily produce gift income for the campaign, this step will alleviate possible future criticism about campaign progress from internal constituents.

External Publications

A good campaign public relations plan should include the use of all appropriate external publications. This may include alumni magazines, messages from the office of the president, newsletters, and other publications designed to inform the external constituents of the college or university.

Consider creating new external publications to keep top volunteers informed on a regular basis. One of these publications might be a confidential campaign document that includes mention of major gifts that have not been announced publicly. This gives volunteers a sense of being campaign insiders and draws them into the process.

Colleges and universities use alumni magazines regularly in spreading the word to alumni and friends about campaign progress.

Establishing a special campaign publication to be mailed to benefactors above a certain giving level can be worthwhile. During The Campaign for Penn State, "Campaign News" was mailed quarterly to 30,000 individuals who gave $250 and above in the current or preceding fund years. This kept the key external philanthropic constituency of the university informed of both campaign priorities and the progress of the campaign.

The Lead Campaign Brochure

The use of a lead campaign brochure is not absolutely vital to the success of the campaign. Some institutions have preferred not to use a lead brochure, seeing it as a waste of institutional funds. They argue that the promotional piece looks good but is seldom read and that most copies end up on a shelf in the basement of the development office.

These arguments notwithstanding, lead brochures are important and serve to validate the campaign. If the campaign devises the lead brochure correctly, it can be used successfully in major gift requests; it should accompany gift proposals routinely.

The following are the key components of a lead campaign brochure.

1. **Opening Statement by the President of the Institution.** Launching a campaign is a very significant event in the life of a college or university. A statement by the president of the institution noting the importance of the campaign is a fundamental element in the brochure. A photograph of the president should accompany the statement.

2. **Statement by the Chairperson of the Campaign.** The chairperson of the campaign must be highly visible throughout the effort. A photograph and statement in the lead brochure help identify the campaign with the chairperson.

3. **Profile of the Chief Academic Officer.** It may be important to profile the chief academic officer of an institution in the lead brochure. This has several benefits, but most importantly it stamps the effort as an academic project and speaks volumes to internal constituents (such as the faculty) about the importance of the academic enterprise. Faculty and students must see the campaign as an academic enterprise. Profiling chief academic officers will lead one to the conclusion that the institution is seeking funds for the most critical academic priorities.

4. **Profiles of Benefactors and Faculty.** It may also be important in the lead brochure to profile prominent faculty as well as major gift benefactors. Select those with whom others can identify, and quote these individuals about their personal as well as institutional views of the importance of the campaign. These profiles can be effective fund-raising "testimonials."

5. **Profiles of Members of the Board of Trustees or Governing Board.** As stated previously, the governing board is critically important to any major enterprise, including a capital campaign. The governing board, particularly at an independent

institution, must "buy into" the process and be integrally involved in every aspect. Profiling certain board members in the lead brochure will draw the board as a whole into the campaign and closely align it with campaign priorities.

6. **Information About the Campaign Goal.** Mention the campaign goal frequently throughout the brochure and break it down into general categories that detail how gifts will be used. A gift range chart should also be included in the brochure to give benefactors a sense of duty and responsibility in making major stretch gifts to the institution.

7. Most campaigns' needs are divided into at least six broad categories, including the following:

   a. *Gifts for Endowment.* This category is generally divided into faculty chairs, professorships, fellowships, and research funds.

   b. *Student Scholarships.* Most capital campaigns include the need for more scholarship funds. Often this category is included along with endowed faculty positions under an endowment category. It may, however, be important to break out the scholarship section from endowed funds for faculty, as this may be more understandable for potential gift prospects.

   c. *New Academic Initiatives.* A goal for some campaigns is to fund important new programs in academic units. These are not necessarily endowed programs but new initiatives that have been identified by the academic officers as highest priorities.

   d. *Institutionwide Objectives.* Many institutions break down their campaign goals by departments or schools of study. There are some projects that have an impact on the total institution, such as the library. It may be important to itemize this area as a separate goal category in order to underscore its importance to the institution as a whole.

   e. *Bricks and Mortar.* Most campaigns set out to raise funds for construction of new buildings and renovation of existing ones.

   f. *Annual Giving.* Comprehensive capital campaigns generally include the total gift support received by an institution during the period of the capital campaign. This will then necessitate a final category for annual gifts that are of an unrestricted, undesignated nature that flow to the institution during the life of the campaign. List a figure in the lead brochure that corresponds to money normally raised during the annual giving program and which does not fall into another funding category.

8. **Specific Ways to Give to the Capital Campaign.** The lead brochure should list specific broad categories with appropriate language so that benefactors can choose the area they wish to benefit. Consider the following:

a. *Named Chairs.* A minimum endowment amount should be listed in the text of the brochure. The highest honor that can be bestowed on a faculty member, the endowed chair, provides an eminent scholar with a salary as well as additional sums to fund graduate assistant salaries, secretarial help, course development, and traveling expenses. An endowed chair is key in attracting and retaining the acknowledged leaders in their fields—the stars of the academic world.

b. *Named Professorships.* The minimum endowment required should be listed in the text. An endowed professorship allows the institution to attract and keep top-flight faculty by supplementing departmental support. Funds are used to provide salary supplements, graduate assistant stipends, secretarial help, and travel expenses. As with named chairs, this kind of support can influence the caliber of faculty an institution is able to recruit as well as the quality of teaching and instruction a department is able to provide.

c. *Endowed Fellowships.* Minimum endowment should be listed in the text. Faculty fellowships allow the institution to provide extra funds to outstanding faculty members. These funds help those who receive them to further their work in teaching, research, and public service. Endowment income goes toward paying graduate assistants, secretarial support, and travel expenses.

d. *Graduate Fellowships.* Minimum endowment should be listed in the lead brochure. To further its mission as a research and teaching institution, a college or university must recruit the brightest graduate students and award them in keeping with their respective needs, responsibilities, and stages of academic development.

e. *Undergraduate Scholarships.* Minimum endowment should be listed in text. A college or university scholarship program has a dual purpose: to attract the most promising students to the institution and to make a college education available to every qualified student, regardless of the individual's background or financial position. Endowed scholarship funds provide the necessary support.

f. *Buildings, Roads, and Plazas.* Where buildings are constructed using private funds, whole buildings or parts of buildings may be named for benefactors. Roads and plazas can also be named. Each instance is individually reviewed in accordance with established institutional policy. Proposed names must be approved by the president of the institution and its governing board.

9. **Gift Acceptance.** A campaign brochure should also explain the process used to make a major commitment to the institution. The brochure should also contain a section on outright gifts and current tax laws relating thereto, including gifts of appreciated securities and real estate.

   A section on deferred gifts and information on how they work should also be contained in the text of the brochure. Include only general information on gift mechanisms in the lead brochure. More technical information should be reserved for other publications that the institution might use in its ongoing development program.

10. **Pledge Form.** The lead brochure should include a pocket or fold-out in the back of the brochure where a pledge form can be placed. The pledge form ought to be kept separate from the body of the brochure to make it easier to use.

11. **Telephone Number and Address.** Finally, a lead brochure should always include a telephone number and address where an interested benefactor can get in touch with campaign officials. Too often, lead campaign brochures do not provide this critical and important information.

Concluding Campaign Brochure

Many institutions use a concluding brochure as a retrospective on the success of the campaign. This publication serves as an historical document and outlines the various successes in the campaign, providing information on major gift support, success at attaining the goal, and information on lead volunteers.

Capital campaigns can change institutions dramatically, and the final campaign brochure provides a vehicle to herald the progress of the institution and the many academic programs affected by a successful campaign. It is also important to list all of the volunteers who were involved in the campaign.

Advertising Plan

Some institutions carry the message of a capital campaign to their key constituents through advertising. This is an often-neglected facet of a campaign as college and university personnel may view advertising as "nonacademic and inappropriate to an academic enterprise." However, advertising is being used increasingly, particularly in announcing major events and campaign progress.

Penn State's $352 million campaign used advertising in two instances. When the original goal was announced, a full-page advertisement was carried in the local newspaper the day after the campaign party announcing the goal. Space was also purchased to list the national campaign committee. At the conclusion of the campaign, a second advertisement was placed in the local newspaper touting the success of the campaign and what it meant to academic programs. The advertisements gave a sense of accomplishment to the immediate university community. Modified versions of these advertisements later ran in internal publications.

College and university advertisements are becoming much more commonplace and more accepted as an important means of communication.

Speakers Bureau

One of the most effective ways to spread the word about a campaign is through a speakers bureau. The speakers bureau puts top university officials and volunteers in front of service clubs, alumni clubs, and constituent groups primarily in close geographic proximity to the institution. These staff members and volunteers speak about the campaign's and direction.

Local service clubs and other groups constantly request speakers for their organizations, and an institution will be one step ahead if it can design a speakers bureau that can accommodate these requests easily and effectively.

The Role of Video in Public Relations

The use of video in capital campaigns has become much more prevalent. While the cost of producing videos is formidable, videos do serve the useful purpose of exciting and informing key constituents.

Videos particularly can be used in the public relations plan to communicate the purpose of the campaign to alumni clubs and service groups, faculty meetings, and student organizations. These videos should be relatively short (7 to 10 minutes), uplifting, and exciting. Consider at least three possible uses of video for campaign public relations purposes:

1. **The Campaign Launch Video.** This video informs viewers of the basic purposes of the campaign and also addresses the mission and challenges facing the institution as a whole. If the video is well produced, it can give constituents a feeling of importance and serve to validate the campaign effort.
2. **Campaign Progress Video.** A video midway through the campaign, showing success in meeting campaign objectives and (perhaps) announcing new goals and objectives, is worth considering. Campaign volunteers are likely to enter a plateau phase during the campaign, and an exciting video praising their successes and highlighting objectives can help to energize the campaign.
3. **Concluding Campaign Video.** This video profiles the campaign achievements as well as key volunteers and benefactors.

Videos can also have tremendous value as keepsakes and cultivation tools for major benefactors. Some institutions even use videos as a form of donor relations, sending benefactors a video anthology with information on endowed scholarships and endowed faculty positions. According to Yale University Vice President Terry Holcombe, this has been a most effective means of communication with major benefactors.

The Role of Video in Fund Raising

A relatively new wave in fund raising is the use of video for gift requests or in conjunction with gift requests through telephone solicitation.[7] The Ohio State University campaign in the late 1980s pioneered the use of video. Ohio State mailed out several thousand videotapes to solicit benefactors for its President's Club. The result was highly successful, and alumni and friends of Ohio State responded well, raising $1,342,900.

Recently, Penn State took the use of video to a new level when attempting to raise $20 million for "an academic/athletic convocation and events center." Major individual and corporate donors committed $15 million of this amount. The campaign then turned to a larger, broad-based audience to attract gifts in the $1,000 to $25,000 range. The goal of this broad-based campaign was $2 million.

The Penn State alumni database contains more than 300,000 alumni and 150,000 "friend" records. Selected from the database were 20,000 individuals who had shown an interest in Nittany Lion athletic programs. Members of the booster organization (the Nittany Lion Club) and former athletes made up the bulk of the target audience for the broad-based video campaign.

Needless to say, it would have been tremendously challenging (if not foolhardy) to ask for gifts of $1,000 to $25,000 over the telephone without a considerable amount of prospect "grooming." Penn State needed to position the convocation center as an important project and build enthusiasm among the targeted audience. Therefore, it mailed three personalized contacts prior to the solicitation. Each contact built upon the previous one with additional information. Meanwhile, the telemarketing group—60 paid Penn State students—attended three special training sessions to build the students' comfort level to ask for gifts of up to $25,000.

A seven-minute videotape was mailed to each of the 20,000 prospects informing them that they would be contacted by a student from Penn State. The videotape outlined the various "ticket packages" for gifts at certain levels and encouraged individuals to qualify for ticket options and/or donor recognition on appropriate plaques to be placed in the new facility.

The response was overwhelming. The total cost of the project was $182,000, and the total raised was $3,440,000. This was a 5.3

cent cost to raise one dollar and exceeded all expectations of the staff. Director of Annual Giving Dan Saftig and Associate Vice President for Development and University Relations Brad Choate, who masterminded the project, believe that telemarketing, combined with a video, can have a dramatic impact on a campaign, provided the audience has been carefully screened and targeted. Saftig and Choate are currently working on another video campaign for endowment support of the university.[8]

Video will be increasingly important, particularly for those institutions with large constituencies. Use of video, when backed up with telephone solicitation, allows an institution to contact many more thousands of alumni with a personalized appeal.

The Campaign Kickoff and Concluding Events

The campaign kickoff and conclusion are celebratory events important to any campaign. Most volunteers and benefactors will want to see a beginning and an ending to the campaign, and those events serve that purpose. According to Roger Williams:

> Special events can inject excitement, spark enthusiasm, and generate momentum in a way that nothing else can approximate. They can introduce, recognize, thank, and motivate volunteers and major donors, communicate key messages about your institution, and dispel myths and misinformation. They can exhilarate participants—and they can be designed as creatively as the imagination will allow.[9]

Heather Ricker Gilbert, a special events consultant, discussed the key to staging a successful campaign kickoff or concluding event. She offered the following advice to development officers:

- Know your purpose. Why are we having this event?
- Understand your audience and situation. Is a black-tie gala appropriate for the culture of your institution?
- Promote a theme that plays up what is special about your institution and its aspirations.
- Create clear and compelling invitations, and mail them at least eight weeks before the event.
- Consider the aesthetics: the food, flowers, decor.

- Analyze the program. What is the best way to showcase key volunteers? Do you need a celebrity, or will a famous alumnus make a better host?
- Rehearse and prepare. Assume nothing, and practice everything possible on site—musicians, sound, lighting, etc.[10]

These campaign events bring together volunteers and major gift benefactors in a special and memorable way. If done properly, benefactors will remember the events as an important time to pause and assess the strengths of their college or university. These events can be marvelous occasions to promote goodwill among internal and external constituents.

Expenses associated with opening and concluding events can be prohibitive for some institutions. Costs of events built around meals are especially exorbitant. Consider sponsoring a reception that would serve light food and perhaps champagne or wine (if alcohol is appropriate) and attempt to avoid the need to feed a large group of friends of the institution.

In The Campaign for Penn State, the opening gala was a large dinner for approximately 1,000 people. Although the event was highly successful, the cost was enormous. In today's environment, an institution could well be criticized for spending institutional funds for such an event.

The concluding gala for The Campaign for Penn State was equally as impressive but not nearly as elaborate or costly. More than 2,000 guests were invited to a reception at the university's hotel complex. Guests then were transported to the university's 2,600-seat auditorium where they were dazzled with a combination of campaign videos, student and faculty performances, and a major Hollywood-style production. The total cost of the concluding event was approximately one-half what a formal sit-down dinner would have cost. Unlike the kickoff, the concluding event was less exclusive and involved more university personnel.

Although cost must always be a factor and extravagance must be avoided, it is important to bring the university community together to experience a cohesiveness of purposes. The campaign opening event and concluding event, if properly staged, can be important occasions to promote the university and the capital campaign.

Board of Governors Resolution

Early in the campaign, the governing board of the college or university should be invited to support the campaign with a formal resolution. This is a good public relations device, and it can receive wide attention among an institution's internal and external groups.

A sample resolution is included in appendix F.

The Recognition Program

The institution must establish donor-recognition guidelines that will become an integral part of the campaign. As Dove points out, "Whether or not people say they want to be recognized, the plain fact is that 99 percent of all people love recognition."[11]

Recognition should be given to benefactors soon after they make major commitments to the campaign. An institution may want to create an overall category of recognition for benefactors who reach a certain cumulative total of giving to the institution. A number of institutions have ongoing gift recognition groups, and there is no reason to cease operating these groups during a capital campaign. The institution may, however, want to raise the level of membership in anticipation of an increased number of people who will be eligible for membership due to the increased activity of a capital campaign. This will help to preserve the aura of "exclusivity."

The following are general guidelines for donor recognition during a capital campaign. The institution should create a recognition program that takes into account the history of the institution, resources available to pay for the recognition program, and the ability to provide staff to conduct the activity.

1. **Donor Recognition for Endowed Chairs and Major Endowment Gifts.** Benefactors who endow chairs, professorships, and other major endowments and/or gifts to capital projects must be recognized with an elegant dinner, hosted by the president of the institution, with appropriate internal and external invited guests. Consider inviting other prospective benefactors to the event for cultivation purposes.

   The president should give the benefactor something tangible—a chair, an engraved plaque, illuminated scroll, or a crystal vase. This recognition helps bond the benefactor to the institution.

2. **Smaller Recognition Events.** Smaller recognition events, including luncheons, meetings with the president, and other university officials would be appropriate for gifts below the major gift level.

3. **Recognition Plaques.** Some institutions create a large plaque that is placed in a highly visible location and which lists all major campaign benefactors. While such recognition is important, it may be impractical for larger institutions with sizable constituencies.

4. **Recognition in Publications.** Recognize major gift benefactors in campaign publications on a continuing, ongoing basis. Many donors appreciate this recognition, and it can also serve as a catalyst for other gifts from individuals who read about the philanthropy of their colleagues. During a campaign there is a tendency to focus on the acquisition of gifts rather than the recognition of generosity. The campaign officers must work hard to avoid this. Recognizing a major gift benefactor during the life of the campaign is very important and should not be overlooked.

Notes

1. Roger L. Williams, "They Work Hard for the Money," in *CASE CURRENTS*: (June 1989): p. 36.
2. Roger L. Williams, "Marketing Begins with Identity," in *Admissions Marketing Report vol. iii no. vii*: (July–August 1987): p. 16.
3. Robert S. Topor, *Institutional Image: How to Define, Improve, Market It.* (Washington, DC: Council for Advancement and Support of Education, 1986), p. 1.
4. Williams, "Marketing Begins with Identity," in *Admissions Marketing Report vol. iii no. vii*: p. 18.
5. Robert L. Krit, *The Fund-Raising Handbook.* (The United States of America: Scott Foresman Professional Books, 1991), p. 159.
6. Roger L. Williams, "The Role of Public Relations in Fund Raising," in *Educational Fund Raising: Principles and Practice.* (Washington, DC: The American Council on Education/Oryx Press, 1993).
7. Jon Van Til and Associates, *Critical Issues in American Philan-*

thropy: Strengthening Theory and Practice. (San Francisco: Jossey-Bass Inc., 1990), p. 50.

8. Leslie S. and Daniel P. Saftig, *Penn State Forever: Endowments at Penn State,* (State College, PA: Filmspace Productions, 1993) [Video].

9. Williams, "The Role of Public Relations in Fund Raising," in *Educational Fund Raising: Principles and Practice.*

10. Heather Ricker Gilbert, "The Winning Combination: When You Put Together Planning and Panache, It Adds Up to a Successful Campaign Special Event," in *CASE CURRENTS*: (June 1989): 42–44.

11. Kent E. Dove, *Conducting a Successful Capital Campaign: A Comprehensive Guide for Nonprofit Organizations.* (San Francisco: Jossey-Bass Inc., 1988), p. 120.

EIGHT

Campaign Accounting

The rush to announce huge campaigns by competing institutions was notorious in the 1980s, and only the declining state of the economy—and perhaps some public criticism—kept mega-campaigns in check during the early 1990s. As the economy begins to pick up steam, competitiveness among colleges and universities to launch large campaigns is, again, evident.

Capital campaigns are now being conducted by hundreds of charities throughout the country. These campaigns do a great deal of good for their respective institutions, but they also tend to fuel a public perception of institutional greed, especially when the mega-campaign is coupled with nationwide reports of tuition hikes outstripping the rate of inflation, and operating budgets threatening deficit spending at some of our most prestigious institutions.

Large endowments at colleges and universities also help to add fuel to this fire, causing the American public to believe colleges and universities have grown too fat, spend too much money, and are financially out of touch with the rest of society. More than 80 percent of the public and independent research universities of the Association of American Universities (AAU) have endowments of more than $100 million. The combined endowments of all AAU institutions total more than $30 billion.[1] The National Institute of Independent Colleges and Universities claims that nearly 55 percent of the 3,500 higher education institutions in the country have endowments under $1 million.[2] Yet, the most sensational sums are readily communicated to the public, causing a perception that the main thing wrong with higher education is that it costs too much.

According to an article in "AGB Reports":

> Not only are we dealing with the perception of huge endowments, but we also face a gross misunderstanding of what an endowment is. Surprisingly, many benefactors and gift prospects who generally are quite sophisticated financially, often know little about endowments. To many, endowments erroneously represent a simple savings account into which an institution can dip its hand at will and extract whatever sum it needs for solving a problem.[3]

This public perception—that colleges and universities are greedy—can be partially offset during a capital campaign by the types of reports that are issued regularly to volunteers, benefactors, and the public at large.

Needs Goal Versus Dollar Goal

Financial reports should track two goals. Obviously, benefactors and volunteers will be very interested in the dollar goal. However, the more important goal of a capital campaign is the achievement of the needs statement. Campaigns are not just about raising money, but raising money for the most critical and important priorities of the institution.

Call for Standard Reporting

Capital campaigns should adhere to stringent guidelines when reporting dollar goals. The Council for Advancement and Support of Education and the National Association of College and University Business Officers promulgated standards for gift accounting that apply to annual reporting several years ago. Most institutions with solid fund-raising programs regularly complete the Council for Aid to Education (CAE) survey of voluntary support of education, which is the only means available nationwide to track gift reporting each year.[4] These reports succinctly define what type gifts to report under prescribed categories.

A blue-ribbon committee of CASE recently promulgated national reporting standards for educational fund-raising campaigns. The committee's conclusion, published as "CASE Campaign Standards: Management and Reporting Standards for Educational Fund

Raising Campaigns," is meant to be a supplement to "Management and Reporting Standards for Educational Institutions: Fund Raising and Related Activities."[5] The latter document provides standard definitions and guidelines on gift valuation but remains silent on the subject of capital campaign accounting and reporting. The author served as a member of the committee and contributed to the promulgation of the standards. This chapter draws heavily from the guidelines and comments on the rationale behind them.

Lack of Uniformity in Campaign Reporting—A National Problem

The final guidelines have been distributed nationwide and should be used by all colleges and universities that conduct capital campaigns. Only through systematic, common reporting guidelines can abuses of the past be eliminated in the future. Higher education needs to ensure that what it is reporting is uniform, consistent, provable, and credible. Colleges and universities that presumably exist to search for truth must be scrupulously honest and fair-minded in their reporting of campaign gifts. Excesses in this regard will only further encourage public perception of institutional greed. Running up campaign totals with revocable gift commitments, verbal pledges, will expectancies, and unsubstantiated commitments will only make faculty, students, alumni, and friends skeptical of the entire development program. Portraying campaigns as successful when they count highly speculative commitments is contrary to everything that higher education is about. Such practices do not accurately reflect the fund-raising performance of the institution. The use of common guidelines will, most assuredly, bring these practices to an end.

The report, "CASE Campaign Standards: Management and Reporting Standards for Educational Fund-Raising Campaigns," is included in appendix M. Some of the rationale behind the standards is included below.

Three Key Concepts

Introduced in the standards are three key concepts that must be seen as fundamental to the overall document. First, campaign reports should separate results of a campaign's featured objectives or needs statement from other institutional purposes. Secondly, campaign reports should separate gifts received during the active campaign solicitation period from gifts the campus expects to get from pledges and other deferred commitments after the campaign ends. Third, campaign reports should give both the face value and the discounted present value of all deferred gifts.

The third key concept, reporting deferred gifts both at face value and discounted present value, was a major compromise that was made in the final negotiation process when the committee met on December 9, 1993. The original draft required that all deferred gifts be discounted to present value, and this caused a tremendous uproar in the profession. At least half of the development professionals throughout the country believed that discounting deferred gifts to present value was not an acceptable way to proceed, and the committee felt that this threatened the survival of the document. The other half believed that present value discounting was the only way to proceed, and anything short of that would be a major compromise to the integrity of the report. As noted in the appendix, the committee decided that a compromise was important in order to resolve the issue and receive maximum acceptance of the campaign guidelines from professionals throughout the country.

The guidelines propose that each college or university conducting a capital campaign will be asked to file a report annually with CASE. This information will be compiled and published annually by CASE as a service to its membership and the public.

This report will provide professionals with a common language for discussing the progress of their capital and major gift campaigns. Institutions will be asked to report their campaigns' financial results in basically three distinct columns. The first will be a reporting of current gifts and pledges at face value. The second will be a reporting of deferred gifts and future commitments reported at face value for featured objectives and other objectives. The third will be a reporting of deferred gifts and future commitments at the gift's discounted present value for featured objectives and other objectives.

This three-column approach is a compromise, a change to the original thinking of the committee. The approach resulted from quite lengthy discussions with a number of professionals and, apparently, was the brainchild of Peter McE. Buchanan, president of CASE. Quoting from the report,

> This multi-column reporting approach is the result of lengthy discussions with CASE members about the pros and cons of reporting deferred gifts (future commitments) at present value versus face value. While discounting to present value represents a substantial change from past practice, many people strongly support its use as a more realistic indicator of the future value those dollars will have when the institution actually is able to spend them. Also, this method accounts for any pay-out obligations to the donor. At the same time, this approach recognizes the concern about the potential negative impact present day discounting could have on donors. When donors make an irrevocable deferred gift, they turn over an asset to the institution and give up their control of it. And, even though the institution may pay back a substantial amount to the donor and will not be able to spend the asset for some time into the future, many donors consider the current face value of the asset as the amount that he or she gave to the institution. Therefore, the standards create three primary reporting columns, plus two columns for totals, to accommodate these concerns. Those who believe that publicly displaying the present value of deferred gifts will, in fact, discourage, donors from making such gifts may choose to report only the first two columns to their constituents, but those institutions should report *all* columns on Appendix B to their appropriate governing boards and to CASE. CASE will in turn report *all* columns in its published report of campaign results. These standards are, therefore, silent on the question of how an institutions should publicly recognize its donors.[6]

This appeared to be a good solution given the difficulty in bringing closure to this important part of the report. CASE will, in turn, report all three columns on an annual basis so that all institutions will be able to compare the their capital campaigns to one another on a level playing field.

Government Funds

During the mid-to-late 1980s, several state legislatures appropriated funds to colleges and universities to create endowments, provided those appropriations could be matched by private commitments. The capital campaign at the University of Minnesota took advantage of this important private/public partnership to increase the university's endowment portfolio dramatically.

After much discussion, the committee, while not criticizing this approach to garnering financial resources, believed that funds that came from legislative appropriation should not be counted in a capital campaign. The matching dollars, of course, could certainly be counted.

Nongovernment Grants and Contracts

Another area of the report that was debated with intensity was nongovernment grants and contracts. Many institutions, particularly major research universities, regularly contract with private industry to perform a variety of research projects. Obviously, as stated in the previous paragraph, publicly supported research dollars in the form of grants and contracts should never be counted in a capital campaign. However, the process of determination becomes complicated when considering privately funded research.

A distinction between grant income and contract revenue must be made but cannot always be determined with ease. The committee's statement on the subject is as follows:

> The difference between a private grant and contract should be judged on the basis of the intention of the awarding agency and the legal obligation incurred by an institution in accepting the award. A grant, like a gift, is bestowed voluntarily and without expectation of any tangible compensation. It is donative in nature. A contract carries an explicit "quid pro quo" between the source and the institution.[7]

Whether this is helpful in deciding what to count and what not to count is not certain. This clause in the standards may, in fact, create more questions and befuddlement than answers and clarification.

It seems that the tangible benefit part of the clause is the most clarifying. If a corporation is receiving a contract for benefit, then it is unlikely that the institution should count those funds in the campaign. There are no easy answers here, and the institution must decide this issue on a case-by-case basis, always leaning in the direction of close scrutiny when reviewing these types of commitments.

Notes

1. G. David Gearhart, R. L. Williams, "Do Mega Campaigns Make Us Look Greedy?" in *AGB Reports vol. 33 no. 1*: (January/February 1992): 17.
2. Gearhart, Williams, "Do Mega Campaigns Make Us Look Greedy?" in *AGB Reports vol. 33 no. 1*: (January/February 1992): 1.
3. Gearhart, Williams, "Do Mega Campaigns Make Us Look Greedy?" in *AGB Reports vol. 33 no. 1*: (January/February, 1992): 1.
4. The Campaign Reporting Advisory Group, Council for Advancement and Support of Education, *CASE Campaign Standards: Management and Reporting Standards for Educational Fund-Raising Campaigns.* (Washington, DC: Council for Advancement and Support of Education, April, 1994).
5. The Campaign Reporting Advisory Group, Council for Advancement and Support of Education, *CASE Campaign Standards: Management and Reporting Standards for Educational Fund-Raising Campaigns*, p. 1.
6. The Campaign Reporting Advisory Group, Council for Advancement and Support of Education, *CASE Campaign Standards: Management and Reporting Standards for Educational Fund-Raising Campaigns*, p. iv.
7. The Campaign Reporting Advisory Group, Council for Advancement and Support of Education, *CASE Campaign Standards: Management and Reporting Standards for Educational Fund-Raising Campaigns*, pp. 9,10.

NINE

Post-Campaign Plan

T he campaign is winding down, the concluding gala has been held, and the volunteers are feeling very good about the success they achieved.

The Challenge Ahead

When the campaign enters its final phase, it is important to undertake an evaluation of the development program and determine its direction during the immediate post-campaign period. The overriding challenge will be to continue the momentum that has been attained in the campaign and sustain the level of private gift support without a campaign context. When a major campaign concludes, the focus and visibility provided by the campaign inevitably change. The case for major gift support becomes more difficult to make, as many benefactors believe that with the successful conclusion of the campaign, programmatic and endowment needs have been met. The academic community may mistakenly believe that the level of resources dedicated to the office of development is no longer necessary. There may even be some individuals who assume that the development program as a whole is no longer necessary, and the campaign has made the need for private gift support in the future a distant priority.

Post-Campaign Objectives

Sustain and Increase Private Giving

To sustain and, indeed, increase the institution's current level of external philanthropic support, the internal and external communities must understand that the efforts and pace of the development program should not decrease once the campaign concludes. All post-campaign planning must be based on the assumption that the primary goal is to simultaneously increase the current level of support while preparing for the next capital campaign.

The primary objective of the development office should be to increase the number of philanthropic dollars. This objective will be achieved by continuing to direct, guide, and participate in the identification, involvement, cultivation, and solicitation of alumni, friends, corporations, foundations, and organizations. However, the campaign should anticipate that total annual support may, in fact, decrease in the immediate years following the campaign. Without the context of a major effort, it is likely that the number of major gifts flowing to the institution will diminish, as will their size. Expect this; it is not an unusual phenomenon. The key is to put in place the staffing, resources, projects, and programs that will maintain total gift support at the highest level possible.

Collaboration with Academic Leadership

While the fundamental goal of the office of development is to increase yearly income, this objective must be pursued in concert with the academic leadership of the institution. Development personnel must make it clear that they provide a service and that the academic leadership of the institution is charged with the responsibility of determining funding priorities. During the campaign, the needs statement listed those priorities. Now that the campaign has ended, a mechanism should be put in place that continues to involve the academic leadership in determining critical priority needs. This requires increased communication with academic officers by members of the development staff. To that end, senior members of the development staff should inaugurate regular planning meetings with academic officials, including deans and academic department heads. These meetings will help to link the fund-raising staff to the academic enterprise.

Evaluation of Needs

The campaign will likely achieve only a percentage of the campaign needs statement. Even though the dollar goal may be surpassed, it is highly unlikely that every need determined early in the campaign will have been met. A needs percentage achievement of 60 or 70 percent is a tremendous accomplishment. In any case, the institution must now initiate a process to establish a new set of needs to help direct the fund-raising agenda once the campaign concludes.

The first step in establishing new needs requires a two-pronged approach:

1. A review of goals and needs that were *not* met in the current campaign
2. The establishment of a new long-term needs statement as determined by the academic leadership of the institution

To initiate the first step, the chief academic officer should ask academic officials to submit a list of those academic needs that are on the current campaign needs statement and were not met during the campaign but are still priorities. These existing unmet needs form the basis for a "revolving" needs statement that will be a fluid document reviewed on an ongoing basis and subject to regular change.

Secondly, the chief academic officer should request that new needs be submitted. Those compiling the new needs ought to take into account the institution's strategic long-range planning process, and should continue to focus on the need to raise endowment support in the form of endowed faculty positions, graduate fellowships, and scholarships—provided this is an area to be targeted as a continuing priority.

Before a need (new or existing) is placed on the revolving needs list, a review should be conducted by the appropriate member of the development staff to determine the fund-raising potential of that particular project. Generally, factors to be considered when reviewing the funding potential of a need are as follows:

1. The overall cost of the project or program as well as the contributed dollars required to support the project
2. The number of identified prospects who may have an interest in that particular project or objective

3. The gift capacity of those prospects and the probable timing of a gift
4. The urgency of the need
5. How each project fits into the overall needs of the institution and its strategic plan

If major needs are identified that might require a heavier institutional commitment (e.g., a major building project), formal feasibility studies should be undertaken to determine the likelihood of success of the project immediately following a major capital campaign.

Focus Campaigns

A natural result of an evolving needs statement will be a decision by the academic leadership to launch a limited number of smaller focus campaigns.[1] A focus campaign may be a project left over from the major capital campaign that was not funded, or it may be one that was not even pursued in the campaign. Focus campaigns are generally efforts that involve the entire constituency of the institution and are built around a project that will benefit that constituency. Examples include a new building project for the library or a classroom building that will be available to all departments and students, or, perhaps, a scholarship fund that benefits every academic unit.

One of the outcomes of the launching of smaller focus campaigns during the off years of a capital campaign is to continue to involve important volunteers in the development program. In addition, many benefactors will have concluded their campaign pledges and may be looking for a project of more limited scope.

Creation of a College or University Development Committee

To facilitate the process of establishing a new needs statement that will represent all areas of the institution and to provide a means of reviewing new initiatives, consider forming a development committee to review major fund-raising projects and to make recommendations to the president and the governing board for those needs that should be funded through focus campaigns. This would be an internal committee composed of representatives of the administration and faculty at the highest levels. This committee should be chaired by the president and should meet on a regular basis. It would be charged with the responsibility of approving focus campaigns as well as the needs statement in the post-campaign environment.

Maintenance of Development Resources

Since the beginning of the campaign, the institution's administration more than likely provided increased funding for the development function. This investment of resources helped to move the campaign forward and probably resulted in an increase in gifts.

To maintain the current level of support as well as to increase private giving in a noncampaign environment, current staffing levels must generally be maintained, and plans must be made to increase or, at the least, maintain the budget of the office of development. Boards and presidents should not decrease the funding of the office of development simply because the campaign has now concluded.[2] Now, more than ever, the development office will need the resources to continue and even increase major gift support. A new level of private gift support has been reached, and it is possible to sustain this level of giving, provided the resources are made available on a continuing basis. Too often, institutions tend to cut the staff of the development office and their annual maintenance budget simply because a campaign has concluded. This is shortsighted and will only lead to a decrease in philanthropic giving in the long run.

Maintenance of Volunteer Programs

One of the most important benefits resulting from a major capital campaign will be the development of a network of volunteers. In a large complex university, these volunteers were probably recruited from throughout the United States, and the participation of new friends and alumni in the institution's affairs is probably at an all-time high. The campaign manager must develop a program to continue involving the most effective of these volunteers once the campaign concludes.

If the institution does not have an ongoing volunteer organizational structure such as a development council, development board, or board of visitors, establish such an organization. Membership could be composed of key campaign volunteers who demonstrated their commitment to philanthropy during the major capital campaign. The purpose of this development board or council would be to provide leadership for major philanthropic activities such as focus campaigns at the university. It would be a mistake to disband the national campaign committee without forming another group that can tap into volunteer leadership.

Reassess Gift Endowment Levels

During the life of the campaign, gift endowment levels were likely maintained. The amounts required to endow a scholarship, professorship, chair, or other program remained constant. The institution would be wise to review these endowment levels and reassess the effectiveness of the income generated. It is possible that managers should increase endowment minimums, and a general review of these amounts should be made before launching another major capital campaign.

Maintenance of Donor/Constituent Relations Program

During the years between campaigns, and prior to a second campaign, a strong constituent/donor-relations program must be maintained. Benefactors must be honored appropriately for major gift support, and continued cultivation is essential to an ongoing development program. Even though a campaign has concluded, the development office is still in the business of raising money for institutional priorities and needs. Alumni and friends of the institution must be made to feel that their gift, after the campaign has concluded, is critically important and deeply appreciated even outside the context of a capital campaign.

Planning for the Next Campaign

As previously stated, many institutions conclude their campaigns and immediately begin planning a second effort to commence in five to seven years. Planning toward that eventuality should begin immediately once the campaign has concluded. A post-campaign committee composed of key development personnel should begin meeting quarterly in anticipation of another campaign. This committee would assess and evaluate the success of the last capital campaign and begin anticipating those elements that will need to be put in place for the next one. To plan for the next campaign is simply to acknowledge reality: fund raising is here to stay in higher education and is likely to play an increasingly important role at both public and independent institutions in the years ahead.

Notes

1. Toni Goodale, "The Ongoing Capital Campaign," in *Fund Raising Management vol. 1 no. 3:* (September 1989): 72.
2. Rita Bornstein, "The Capital Campaign: Benefits and Hazards," in James L. Fisher and G.H. Quehl ed., *The President and Fund Raising,* (New York: American Council on Education and Macmillan Publishing Company, 1989) pp. 202–211.

Appendix A

_____
Interviewee

FEASIBILITY STUDY
(College or University Name)

1.   Does the College/University enjoy a positive image in the community?

    a.   How would you rank the educational programs of the College or University?

        1.   Excellent
        2.   Good
        3.   Fair
        4.   Don't Know/No Opinion

    b.   How would you rate the administration of the College or University?

    c.   How would you rate the faculty of the College/University?

    d.   How would you rate the fund-raising programs at the College/University)?

2.   Do you believe that the building of a new facility for the College/University is a priority for the State of   ?

159

3.   Is the College/University responsive to community and professional needs?

4.   How do you compare the College/University to other comparable institutions?

5.   Do you consider the College/University an important community and regional asset? In what ways?

6.   The new facility is being financed by a combination of state and University funds. In anticipation of the completion of this facility, the College/University wishes to launch an endowment program to strengthen educational programs. Potential benefactors will be asked to contribute to an endowment fund for a variety of purposes including scholarships, lectureships, endowed chairs, and professorships. These funds will greatly enhance the educational mission of the College/University. In recognition of gifts from benefactors, areas within the new building will be named for gifts at appropriate levels. Do you consider this project to be both important and urgent?

7.   One million dollars to three million dollars has been estimated as the total dollar goal for this campaign. In your opinion, can the College/University raise $1 million to $3 million from the private sector in a campaign?

8.   What is the most that you believe the College/University could raise for this project?

9. In this campaign, it is anticipated that most of the funds raised will come from a small number of major gifts. In a campaign of the scale we are discussing here, commitments in the $25,000 to $100,000 range and up will be required for success. In fact, we are hoping that we might be able to secure some gifts as high as $250,000 to $1 million. Keeping in mind that gifts can be cash, securities, and real estate and can be fulfilled over a five-year pledge term, would you be willing to suggest to me the names of individuals, corporations, and foundations that you think have the ability and possible interest to make such gifts to this campaign?

10. If you were to be called upon to assist with this project by making a gift, would you have interest in the project?

11. I would like to ask you to share with me, on a strictly confidential basis, the giving level that you might consider for this project if financial circumstances are right and an appealing naming opportunity in the new building is placed before you?

12. Who do you believe would be an important and critical volunteer to the success of this fund-raising project?

13. Would you be willing to be a part of the campaign as a volunteer?

14.   Is the timing right to launch a campaign of this magnitude?

15.   Where does this project fit into your civic priorities on a scale from one to ten, with one being the highest?

16.   Is there any reason by the College/University should not embark upon a campaign of this magnitude as soon as it is prepared to do so?

17.   Are there any other matters bearing on this project that you feel should be addressed prior to embarking on a campaign for the College/University?

Appendix B

COLLEGE OF THE LIBERAL ARTS NEEDS STATEMENT

A society prospers and endures when its people are rich in imagination, insight, and critical inquiry. Penn State's College of the Liberal Arts helps foster these intellectual skills by providing the knowledge of human experience, of values, and of cultural traditions.

The 1985 Association of American Colleges' report on the meaning and purpose of baccalaureate education defined the ability to communicate ideas with precision and clarity as a primary goal of postsecondary education. Mastery of our own and of foreign languages enables students to use their skills of analysis and inquiry. By integrating liberal education with professional studies, students are prepared to apply their knowledge in diverse settings.

In the College of the Liberal Arts, faculty are devoted to helping students gain a mastery of language, an awareness of private and social values, and knowledge of the diversity of cultures and experiences that define the contemporary world. The faculty includes distinguished scholars who have developed programs recognized for their excellence.

The college is a national leader in foreign language pedagogy. A satellite system for receiving foreign language broadcasts and specially designed classrooms provide the latest techniques and technology for language instruction.

The Department of Philosophy's faculty is internationally prominent in scholarship and also is highly active in instruction on Penn State's Commonwealth Campuses. The Department of Speech Communication's graduate program has been ranked among the top three in the country. Its alumni include two college presidents.

A team of psychology faculty studies the relationship between emotions and wellness. The expertise of this research group, which includes Evan Pugh Professor Herschel W. Liebowitz, is unequalled anywhere in the world. Industrial/organizational psychologists are bringing their skills to institutional and corporate settings to improve employee and management operations far beyond the University.

The National Endowment for the Humanities has recognized and supported the college's commitment to excellence through a challenge grant, the largest award NEH made in 1985. By successfully raising $3 million in new and increased private support over the next three years, the college will receive $1 million from NEH.

To enhance its level of excellence, Penn State's College of the Liberal Arts is seeking $7.75 million for academic program support. The money would be used for the following purposes:

— $5.25 million for faculty support. Endowed faculty chairs in Literary Theory and Comparative Criticism, Ethics, and Anglo-German Literary Relations would build on programs of distinction and use resources unique to Penn State, such as the Allison-Shelley Collection of Anglo-German translations. Endowed professorships would be established in newly developing disciplines — Women's Studies, Group and Organizational Communications, Clinical/Industrial Psychology, and Jewish Life and Literature. An endowed Visiting International Professorship would aim to bring the best of the world's scholars to the college. A Research and Development Fund would help provide critically needed resources for college faculty.

— $1 million for student aid. Outstanding graduate students are crucial for the college to achieve excellence in research and teaching. The quality of future faculty depends on attracting top students to graduate study. Critical shortages of outstanding faculty are beginning to develop. The college's responsibility to excellence in the future requires assistance to attract the nation's best students.

— $1.5 million for program enhancements. The money would be used to enhance the college's first-rate writing program and will fund a major television series based on the work of Penn State's prominent archaeologists. A Resident Writers Program would complement the faculty by providing for extended visits by the nation's leading scholars. The Department of English is the largest in the country, and its faculty includes several of the nation's outstanding writers. Faculty members Stanley Weintraub and Philip Young hold the Evan Pugh Professorship. The Department of Anthropology is bringing archaeology's newest approaches and techniques to the public through a nationally televised course titled "New Directions." Two of its faculty, William T. Sanders and Paul T. Baker, are members of the National Academy of Sciences and hold Evan Pugh Professorships.

L Ed 87-808

Produced by the Penn State Department of Publications

COLLEGE OF BUSINESS ADMINISTRATION NEEDS STATEMENT

Already recognized as one of the nation's top business schools, Penn State's College of Business Administration is poised to assume a position of even greater national and international leadership in the study of management and business administration.

Through innovative approaches to teaching and research, the college is keeping pace with the rapidly changing world of business. Anticipating those changes, the college's Division of Research has established seven centers for research. Each unit deals with an area that is critical to the future of American business: strategic decision making; the management of technological and organizational change; pension and welfare research; regional business analysis; the study of business markets; issues management research; and real estate studies.

The college includes seven departments, which provide a focus for the study of business disciplines. Several departments have been recognized for outstanding achievement. Studies of the impact of strategic decisions on the financial community have been sponsored by the Blankman Program and have brought recognition to the Department of Finance. Activities associated with the William Elliott Program and Chair annually bring leaders of the insurance industry to Penn State. With its emphasis on the study of business markets, the Department of Marketing plays a unique role among universities studying in this area. Accounting and Business Logistics are internationally noted as outstanding departments, with Business Logistics recently ranked by two independent surveys as the top program in the nation.

Professional programs at the M.B.A. and executive education levels have attained national and international prominence. The executive education program is regularly cited as among the best in the land, and in a recent survey, Penn State's was ranked among the top three, along with those of Harvard and Stanford. The college's M.B.A. program is considered one of the country's top twenty and is rated as one of the most rapidly improving M.B.A. programs in the nation.

Other innovative programs are being launched as well. The G. Albert Shoemaker Program in Business Ethics provides an examination of management ethics and corporate social responsibility. The program includes lectures, conferences, panel discussions, and research studies designed to affect the entire business curriculum. The Shoemaker Program is one of the first of its kind.

To enhance this level of excellence, Penn State's College of Business Administration is seeking $6.4 million for academic program support. The money would be used for the following purposes:

— $4 million for faculty support. Endowed chairs, professorships, and University fellowships would provide the faculty leadership needed to develop outstanding programs, student activities and curricula in the core disciplines of the college. Competition for top faculty in business administration is intense, and this type of support is essential for developing excellent programs that enable students to learn from outstanding teachers.

— $1.1 million for student aid. Gifts to this area would be used for fellowships, grants, and scholarships for both undergraduate and graduate students. This support would attract the best and brightest students at all levels and reward outstanding performance among those already enrolled.

— $1.3 million for capital construction and program enhancement. Of this, $1 million would fund construction of the Management Education Laboratory, which would house special classrooms that simulate a working business environment. In addition, funds are needed to support special programs and centers to enable the college to be on the cutting edge of studying and examining national issues.

The Pennsylvania State University, in compliance with federal and state laws, is committed to the policy that all persons shall have equal access to programs, admission, and employment without regard to race, religion, sex, national origin, handicap, age, or status as a disabled or Vietnam-era veteran. Direct all affirmative action inquiries to the Affirmative Action Officer, Suzanne Brooks, 201 Willard Building, University Park, PA 16802; (814) 863-0471.

U.Ed. 87-802

Produced by the Penn State Department of Publications

COLLEGE OF ENGINEERING NEEDS STATEMENT

For more than a century, Penn State's College of Engineering has been Pennsylvania's single greatest source of engineering graduates. Since the turn of the century, the college has ranked among the top ten institutions in the country in the number of students enrolled in its baccalaureate program.

In fact, one in every fifty engineers in the nation with a bachelor's degree earned that degree from Penn State.

Throughout its history, the college has been an innovative force in engineering education nationwide. In 1909, it became the first college in the nation to offer a degree program in industrial engineering. The college also initiated the first formal program in engineering extension, which later developed into the University's Commonwealth Campus System.

With the creation of an Engineering Experiment Station in 1909, Penn State became one of America's first academic institutions involved in engineering research. In the last five years alone, the college has more than doubled its sponsored research expenditures, to the tune of more than $15 *million* in 1985–86.

The college's Breazeale Nuclear Reactor was one of the first college or university research reactors to be licensed by the Atomic Energy Commission. Recently relicensed by the Nuclear Regulatory Commission, it is the nation's longest-operating university reactor.

However, sheer numbers and being a pioneer do not tell the entire story. Even more impressive is the quality of the graduates produced by the College of Engineering.

More than one hundred forty chief or senior executive officers of Fortune 1000 corporations are among the 50,000 Penn State engineering alumni.

Three engineering alumni are astronauts. Paul Weitz, a 1954 aeronautical engineering graduate, piloted the first flight of the shuttle Challenger in 1983. Captain Weitz also flew on a 1973 Skylab mission. Colonel Guion Bluford, a 1964 aerospace engineering graduate, was a mission specialist on Challenger flights in 1983 and 1985. He is the nation's first black astronaut. Robert Cenker, a 1970

aerospace engineering graduate who also holds a master's degree in aerospace engineering from Penn State, was a payload specialist on the January 1986 flight of the shuttle Columbia.

To enhance the level of excellence that makes such accomplishments possible, Penn State's College of Engineering is seeking $21.05 million for academic program support. The funds would be used for the following purposes:

— $6.95 million for faculty support. This would include three endowed chairs in thrust areas of engineering education and research that are critical to the country's needs; fifteen professorships throughout the various engineering programs; and faculty fellowships in Electrical Engineering and Mechanical Engineering. Competition for top engineering faculty is intense, and such support is necessary if the college is to attract and retain quality professors. The endowed chairs are meant to attract key faculty with internationally recognized expertise in critical areas, while the professorships would broaden the base of faculty quality by attracting new senior-level professors.

— $3.6 million for student aid. The opportunity to work with superior students attracts and retains superior faculty. Important research is conducted by students under the supervision of such faculty. Scholarships and fellowships help to bring the brightest engineering students to Penn State and encourage them to continue at the University in graduate programs. This, in turn, increases the talent pool from which new faculty can be appointed.

— $5.5 million for program enhancement. Because engineering technologies constantly are changing, it is critical that the College of Engineering keep pace. The money would provide for the purchase of additional equipment that will keep laboratories up-to-date. In addition, innovative Centers of Excellence in Research and Instruction are planned, to further enhance the college's level of excellence in these two areas.

— $5 million for facilities expansion and improvement. Additional funds are required to complete capital building projects that are funded only partially by the Commonwealth. A number of vital new facilities are needed as well.

The Pennsylvania State University, in compliance with federal and state laws, is committed to the policy that all persons shall have equal access to programs, admission, and employment without regard to race, religion, sex, national origin, handicap, age, or status as a disabled or Vietnam-era veteran. Direct all affirmative action inquiries to the Affirmative Action Officer, Suzanne Brooks, 201 Willard Building, University Park, PA 16802; (814) 863-0471.

U Ed. 87-806

Produced by the Penn State Department of Publications

Appendix C

University Named Chairs - Minimum endowment: $1 million

The highest honor that can be bestowed on a faculty member, the endowed chair provides an eminent scholar with a salary, as well as additional sums to fund graduate assistant salaries, secretarial help, course development, and traveling expenses. An endowed chair is key in attracting and retaining the acknowledged leaders in their fields--the stars of the academic world.

University Named Professorships - Minimum endowment: $250,000

An endowed professorship allows the University to attract--and to keep--top-flight faculty, by supplementing departmental support. Funds are used to provide salary supplements, graduate assistant stipends, secretarial help, and travel expenses. As with named chairs, this kind of support can influence the caliber of faculty we are able to recruit, as well as the quality of teaching and instruction a department is able to provide.

University Endowed Fellowships - Minimum contribution: $100,000

Faculty fellowships allow the University to provide extra funds to outstanding faculty members. These funds help those who receive them to further their work in teaching, research, and public service. Endowment income goes toward paying graduate assistants, secretarial support, and travel expenses.

Graduate Fellowships - Minimum contribution: $50,000

To further its mission as a great research and teaching institution, College/University must recruit the brightest graduate students and reward them in keeping with their respective needs, responsibilities, and stages of academic development.

Undergraduate Scholarships

The College/University scholarship program has a dual purpose: to attract the most promising students to the University and to make a University education available to every qualified student, regardless of the individual's background or financial position. Endowed scholarship funds provide the necessary support.

There are three ways to institute a named scholarship:

A.   A gift of $25,000. A gift of $25,000 or more will be used to fund an Academic Excellence Scholarship. As a specially targeted area of scholarship funding within the Campaign, this premier scholarship is offered to students who are invited to participate in the College/University University Scholars Program.

B.   A gift of $15,000. A gift of $15,000 or more is used to establish a separate endowment fund scholarship. The donor is free to establish selection requirements for those receiving the scholarship, provided the established terms fall within the law and do not unreasonably restrict the scholarship.

C.   A gift of $10,000. A gift of at least $10,000 can be used to establish a named scholarship in one of four already existing University endowed scholarship programs. These cover the areas of greatest need for scholarship support. Separate guidelines have been established for each of these programs.

   i.   Alumni Memorial Scholarship. These scholarships are awarded on merit, to recruit students of the highest caliber.

   ii. College/University National Merit Scholars Scholarship. Selection for these scholarships is based on procedures administered by the National Merit Scholarship Corporation.

   iii. College/University National Achievement Scholars Scholarship. These scholarships are awarded to black students selected under the National Achievement Scholars Program of the National Merit Scholarship Corporation.

   iv. Renaissance Scholarship. These are awarded to the "brightest of the neediest" students.

Appendix D

Sound off

Sound off *is your chance to share an opinion about* CASE *areas of interest. Send manuscripts for consideration to* CASE CURRENTS, *Suites 530/600, One Dupont Circle, Washington, DC 20036.*

58

Name that campaign

BY BERNICE A. THIEBLOT
President
The North Charles Street Design Organization

Illustration by Susan Davis

Inflation has proven to be an ill wind blowing a beneficial side effect to fund raisers and publications consultants. As endowments are ravaged, capital campaigns are springing up like crocuses. And inventing those words and phrases that sear minds, kindle dreams, and open hearts and checkbooks has once again emerged as an art form.

Based on recent experience, I am convinced that the most difficult activity associated with a campaign—second only to raising the money itself—is naming it.

Because finding a name is so taxing, too many institutions are copping out—resorting to campaigns designated by numbers. You'll recognize them by such names as "Eighty Million for the Eighties" or "Two Centuries: Two Million." Numbers lack the power to stir souls. Better, we think, to name a campaign for its philosophical objectives and attain a loftiness beyond measurement.

In the interest of serving higher education, we have developed our own patented method for naming campaigns which we, herewith, share with you.

Using this system is as simple as ordering from a Chinese menu. Notice that there are three columns. Begin by reading down Column A until you find the participle or infinitive that seems most appropriate to your campaign. Next, choose the phrase from Column B that feels just right. All you need is a noun from Column C and, presto, your campaign has the perfect name.

(For example, if you had chosen #30 in Column A, #18 in Column B, and #43 in Column C, you would have "Mandate for an Extraordinary Personal Sacrifice." Now what could describe the objectives of a capital campaign better than that?)

A word of caution to the novice: Beware the acronym. "Advancement of a Superb Structure" will not do. Neither will "Signalling an Abundance of Progress." CASE

Column A	Column B	Column C
Toward	Greater	Endowment
Honoring	a Tradition of	Learning
Quest for	a Commitment to	Quality
Time for	a Heritage of	Enrichment
In Support of	the Enrichment of	Leadership
Celebrating	a Century of	Service
Opportunity for	a Larger	Purpose
Creating	a More Perfect	Wisdom
To Share	an Ancient	Gift
Burnishing	a Hallmark of	Tradition
Program for	a Keystone of	Greatness
Investment in	a Foundation of	Abundance
Glorifying	a Fount of	Beneficence
Exalting	the Margin of	Excellence
Transcending	the Maghitude of	Vision
Signalling	an Abundance of	Progress
Force for	a Remarkable	Imperative
Imperative for	an Extraordinary	Decade
Affirming	a Lofty	Achievement
Frontier of	a Noble	Dream
In Search of	a Mighty	Fulfillment
Pursuit of	an Illustrious	History
To Perpetuate	a Signal	Honor
To Sustain	a Renowned	Presence
Advancement of	a Glorious	Difference
Fulfilling	a Grand	Development
Surpassing	a Majestic	Promise
The Consummation of	a Perpetual	Campaign
Campaign for	a Legacy of	Service
Mandate for	a Superb	Idea
Reinforcing	a Peerless	Covenant
Building	a Monument to	Philanthropy
Maximizing	Matchless	Money
Uniting	a Superior	Structure
Resources for	the Vastness of	Opportunity
Optimizing	an Enduring	Edifice
Counterbalancing	the Strife of	Inflation
Generating	the Elements of	Accountability
Engineering	an Edifice for	Excellence
Ennobling	a Capacity for	Generosity
Upgrading	the Frequency of	Investment
Motivating	the Occurrence of	Giving
Strengthening	a Generous	Personal Sacrifice
Chiseling	a Monument to	Expansion
Forging	a Vital	Link
Renewing	an Unbroken Chain of	Promises
Reaffirming	a Tower of	Truth
Signalling	a New Age of	Unity
Safeguarding	a Vision of	Virtue
Articulating	a Gracious	Prominence
To Cultivate	an Enduring	Vitality
Reaping	the Rewards of	Industry
Preserving	a Viable	Alternative

S O U N D   O F F

NAME THAT CAMPAIGN II

Nomenclature in the '90s: 343,000 possibilities for your next fund drive

BY BERNICE ASHBY THIEBLOT

Thieblot

When CURRENTS asked me to update my March 1979 look at campaign slogans, I couldn't help noticing that the campaigns of this decade have evolved. Today's drive is more ambitious than its predecessor—longer and more comprehensive. And whether or not the campaign focuses on an institutional anniversary, it's more likely to acknowledge the coming turn of the century.

Certain things, though, have not changed. A campaign still needs a memorable, thematic name—and it's still just as likely not to have one. If anything, today's larger, more amorphous efforts have names that are duller than ever.

My original "Name That Campaign" posited an alternative—a chart that let you try my personal formula for crafting that all-important capital campaign moniker. Today's new priorities and language suggest it's time to update the terms of 15 years ago.

Using this naming system is as easy as ordering from a Chinese menu. Simply scan the columns, select the terms that seem appealing, and presto—your campaign has a name. If you choose Nos. 43, 29, and 55, for example, you'll have "Mandate for an Extraordinary Personal Sacrifice" (a favorite of mine). If you bypass the appetizer and choose only from columns B and C, Nos. 56 and 26 give you "A Monument to Meaning" (which is certainly timely).

Some combinations work better than others, of course. (Beware the unfortunate acronym—"Advancing a Spirit of Service," for example.) Even so—and without counting the variations you can achieve by switching gerunds to infinitives, changing singulars to plurals, and swapping the articles "a" and "the"—there are 343,000 combinations here. You may find the right name for your campaign, one worthy of the coming millennium. ◼

Bernice Ashby Thieblot heads the North Charles Street Design Organization in Baltimore.

COLUMN A	COLUMN B	COLUMN C
1. To Structure	A New	Paradigm
2. Milestones Toward	A Magnificent	Millennium
3. Innovating	A Global	Interface
4. Transforming	A Spirited	Ideal
5. To Perpetuate	Traditional	Values
6. To Harness	A Vast	Technology
7. Envisioning	A Vision of	Vision
8. Toward	A Greater	Endowment
9. To Honor	A Tradition of	Learning
10. Advancing	Advanced	Advances
11. Quest for	A Commitment to	Quality
12. Time for	A Heritage of	Innovation
13. In Support of	The Enrichment of	Leadership
14. To Celebrate	A Century of	Service
15. Opportunity for	A Spirit of	Resolve
16. To Create	A More Perfect	Archetype
17. To Bestow	A More Purposeful	Purpose
18. To Share	An Ancient	Gift
19. To Burnish	A Bold	Tradition
20. Program for	A Keystone of	Greatness
21. Investment in	A Foundation of	Abundance
22. Glorifying	Access to	Beneficence
23. Exalting	The Margin of	Excellence
24. Transcending	The Magnitude of	Progress
25. Achieving	An Eminent	Institution
26. Signaling	An Abundance of	Meaning
27. Force for	A Remarkable	Imperative
28. Access to	A More Accessible	Access
29. Imperative for	An Extraordinary	Decade
30. To Honor	Another	Century
31. In Search of	Our Greatest	Strengths
32. To Affirm	A Lofty	Achievement
33. Frontier of	A Noble	Dream
34. Pursuit of	An Illustrious	History
35. Resolving	A Mighty	Fulfillment
36. To Perpetuate	A Signal	Honor
37. To Sustain	A Renowned	Presence
38. Enhancing	A Glorious	Difference
39. Fulfilling	A Grand	Development
40. To Surpass	A Majestic	Promise
41. Continuing	A Perpetual	Campaign
42. Campaign for	A Legacy of	Wisdom
43. Mandate for	A Superb	Idea
44. Reaffirming	A Peerless	Covenant
45. Building	Caring	Philanthropy
46. Maximizing	Matchless	Money
47. To Unite	A Superior	Structure
48. Resources for	The Vastness of	Opportunity
49. To Maintain	An Enduring	Edifice
50. Engineering	An Edifice for	Edification
51. Ennobling	A Capacity for	Generosity
52. Billions for	A Breathtaking	Bimillennial
53. Safeguarding	A Splendid	Investment
54. Providing	The Occurrence of	Giving
55. Strengthening	A Generous	Personal Sacrifice
56. Chiseling	A Monument to	Expansion
57. To Forge	A Vital	Link
58. To Renew	An Unbroken Chain of	Promises
59. Restoring	A Tower of	Truth
60. Extending	A New Age of	Unity
61. To Seek	Two Centuries of	The Future
62. Pledging	A World of	Change
63. Preserving	The Elements of	Virtue
64. To Dream of	A Gracious	Prominence
65. To Cultivate	The Rewards of	Vitality
66. Keeping Viable	A Viable	Alternative
67. Fostering	A Meaningful	Legacy
68. Sharing	A Momentous	Bond
69. Progress Toward	A Significant	Venture
70. To Champion	A Notable	Enterprise

Appendix E

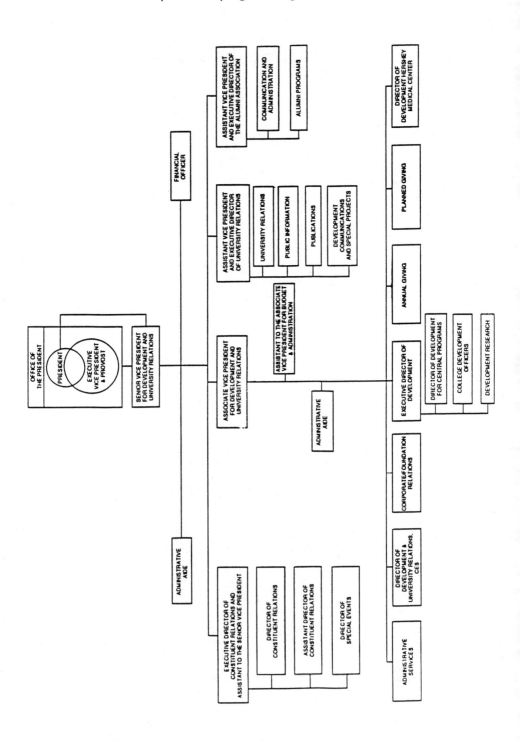

Appendix F

Board of Trustees
9/12/86   105-6

Remarks by Mr. William A. Schreyer, Chairman, The Campaign for Penn State

Following remarks regarding The Campaign for Penn State, Mr. William A. Schreyer, Chairman, acknowledged the tremendous efforts being put forth by everyone involved with the Campaign -- the staff, the volunteer leadership, the members of the Executive Committee, the members of the National Campaign Committee, and all those persons who have committed their time or resources to the Campaign. Mr. Schreyer introduced the Campaign Vice Chairmen -- Edward R. Hintz, Joseph V. Paterno and Frank P. Smeal and the Campaign Treasurer, Robert E. Eberly, Sr. He recognized the honorary members of the Campaign Committee -- Trustee Emeriti Hallowell, Shoemaker and Ulerich.

Mr. Schreyer read a letter from Governor Dick Thornburgh conveying his best wishes for a successful fundraising campaign. (Letter on file in the Office of the Board of Trustees.)

Mr. Schreyer presented for the trustees' approval the following resolution endorsing the goal of The Campaign for Penn State:

WHEREAS, The Campaign for Penn State is critical to attaining the University's overarching goal as identified by the strategic planning process "to secure its status among the best public research universities in the nation";

WHEREAS, the University has generated a six-fold increase in private support over the last decade, from $5.8 million in 1975-76 to $37.6 million in 1985-86;

WHEREAS, the University has performed especially well in attracting corporate gift support over the years, attracting nearly twice the national average in corporate giving to higher education institutions (41 percent of Penn State's total gift support derived from corporations in 1985-86);

WHEREAS, total private gift support to higher education increased 13 percent in 1984-85 to a record $6.3 billion, indicating a favorable economic climate for fund raising;

WHEREAS, the University has attracted excellent voluntary leadership to spearhead The Campaign for Penn State; and

WHEREAS, the Campaign priorities identified by the University's academic officers have been endorsed by all appropriate bodies;

THEREFORE, BE IT RESOLVED, That the Board of Trustees of The Pennsylvania State University approves the monetary goal of The Campaign for Penn State as will be announced by the Campaign Executive Committee on September 13, 1986, and extends its warm support and encouragement to the Committee in this most important challenge.

The Board of Trustees approved the above resolution unanimously.

Appendix G

Campaign II

Years

Task Name	1992	1993	1994	1995	1996	1997	1998	1999	2000	2001	2002	2003	20
IDENTIFY ADVANCED GIFT PROSPECTS													
DEVELOP PRELIMINARY PLAN													
DEVELOP OPERATIONS PLAN													
FORMULATE CASE													
DEVELOP PLAN FOR INVOLVING ALUMNI ASSN													
DEVELOP PUBLIC RELATIONS PLAN													
LEADERSHIP RECRUITMENT													
ADVANCED GIFT SOLICITATIONS													
Start Counting													
Solicit the Committee													
Solicit the Trustees													
COUNT GIFTS													
PREPARE PUBLIC CAMPAIGN MATERIALS													
PUBLIC CAMPAIGN PERIOD													
Public Announcement													
Major Gifts Phase													
Conduct Faculty Staff Campaign													
Broad Based Campaign													
Campaign Gala													

Appendix H

ALUMNI/DEVELOPMENT DATA SYSTEM COMPANIES

Vendor	Address
Access International, Inc.	432 Columbia Street Cambridge, MA 02141
Advocate Development Corporation	891 Montvale Avenue Stoneham, MA 02180
Blackbaud, Inc.	4401 Belle Oaks Drive Charleston, SC 29405-8530
Business Systems Resources, Inc.	1000 Winter Street, Suite 1200 Waltham, MA 02154
Datatel, Inc.	4375 Fair Lakes Court Fairfax, VA 22033
Information Associates, Inc.	3000 East Ridge Road Rochester, NY 14622
Iowa System for Institutional Advancement, Inc.	180 North Riverside Drive Post Office Box 2808 Iowa City, IA 52244-2808
PG Calc Incorporated	129 Mount Auburn Street Cambridge, MA 02138
Quodata Corporation	One Union Place Hartford, CT 06103
Jeffery R. Shy Associates, Inc.	4732 East Long Hill Road Williamsburg, VA 23188
Systems & Computer Technology Corporation	4 Country View Road Malvern, PA 19355
TARGET/1 Management Systems	27 Millett Drive Auburn, ME 04210
Viking Systems, Inc.	25 Church Street Boston, MA 02116

Appendix I

Sample Gift Chart   **Goal: $10,000,000**

Number of Gifts Needed	In the Range of	Total for the Range	Cumulative Total	Number of Prospects Required
1	$2,000,000	$2,000,000	$2,000,000	5
2	$1,000,000	$2,000,000	$4,000,000	10
3	$500,000	$1,500,000	$5,500,000	15
4	$250,000	$1,000,000	$6,500,000	20
10	$100,000	$1,000,000	$7,500,000	50
20	$50,000	$1,000,000	$8,500,000	100
30	$25,000	$750,000	$9,250,000	150
50	$10,000	$500,000	$9,750,000	250
Many	< $10,000	$250,000	$10,000,000	Many

Sample Gift Chart   **Goal: $100,000,000**

Number of Gifts Needed	In the Range of	Total for the Range	Cumulative Total	Number of Prospects Required
1	$20,000,000	$20,000,000	$20,000,000	5
1	$10,000,000	$10,000,000	$30,000,000	5
2	$5,000,000	$10,000,000	$40,000,000	10
4	$3,000,000	$12,000,000	$52,000,000	20
6	$1,000,000	$6,000,000	$58,000,000	30
10	$500,000	$5,000,000	$63,000,000	50
30	$250,000	$7,500,000	$70,500,000	150
50	$100,000	$5,000,000	$75,500,000	250
100	$50,000	$5,000,000	$80,500,000	500
200	$25,000	$5,000,000	$85,500,000	1000
500	$10,000	$5,000,000	$90,500,000	2500
Many	< $10,000	$9,500,000	$100,000,000	Many

Appendix J

INVESTMENT COMMITMENT
FOR CAPITAL PROJECTS

In consideration of my interest in education and for and in consideration of the similar promises of other donors, and to induce others to contribute to _____ College/University and in consideration of the University's promise to use this gift as specified herein and the University's actions in reliance on this pledge, and other good and valuable consideration, the receipt of which is hereby acknowledged, and intending to be legally found hereby, I/we hereby pledge and promise to pay to _____ College/University the sum of $_____.

This gift will be used for _____
_____ and this promise to use
and the use by the University of the amount pledged shall in itself constitute full and adequate consideration for this pledge.

This commitment will be paid to _____ College/University in the following manner:

PLEDGE YEAR 1 $_____

PLEDGE YEAR 2 $_____

PLEDGE YEAR 3 $_____

PLEDGE YEAR 4 $_____

PLEDGE YEAR 5 $_____

_____ Total amount for this year's gift is enclosed.

_____ I/We prefer to make the annual gifts in the month of _____, beginning 19__.

_____ Additional funds will be forthcoming through matching gifts from my company or my spouse's company which is

_____
(Company Name)

_____ The above pledge will include matching gifts from my company or my spouse's company which is

_____
(Company Name)

This pledge is to be irrevocable and a binding obligation upon me, my estate, my executors and my heirs. This pledge shall be governed and interpreted under the laws of the State or Commonwealth of _____. In witness I/we hereby sign and seal this Pledge Agreement with the intention to be legally bound hereby.

_____   _____
Signature   Date

_____   _____
Signature   Date

Please acknowledge and credit this gift in the following way:

_____

Name(s) (please print)

_____

Street

_____

City, State, Zip Code

Please make checks payable to:
_____ College or University

THE PLEDGE YEAR runs from
July 1 through June 30.
LCBP

Pledge Accepted By:
Office of University Development
_____ COLLEGE OR UNIVERSITY
Street Address
City, State   Zip Code

_____
Staff Representative

_____
University Officer

185

Appendix K

INVESTMENT COMMITMENT IN
THE _____ COLLEGE OR UNIVERSITY

To make a commitment to The _____ College or University, I/we register a total gift/pledge of $_____

This gift will be used for:

This commitment will be paid to The _____ College or University in the following manner:

PLEDGE YEAR 1 $_____

PLEDGE YEAR 2 $_____

PLEDGE YEAR 3 $_____

PLEDGE YEAR 4 $_____

PLEDGE YEAR 5 $_____

_____ Total amount for this year's gift is enclosed.

_____ I/We prefer to make the annual gifts in the month of _____, beginning 19___.

I/We prefer to make this gift in the following manner:

_____ Cash Securities, or Real Property   _____ Charitable Trust
_____ Life Insurance   _____ Gift Annuity
_____ Pooled Income Fund   _____ Other (please specify)
                                                _____

_____ Additional funds will be forthcoming through matching gifts from my company or my spouse's company which is

_____
Company Name

_____   _____
Signature   Date

_____   _____
Signature   Date

Please acknowledge and credit this gift in the following way:

_____
Name(s) (please print)

_____
Street

_____
City, State, Zip Code

Please make checks payable to:
_____ College or University

THE PLEDGE YEAR runs from
July 1 through June 30.

Pledge Accepted By:
Office of University Development
_____ COLLEGE OR UNIVERSITY
Street Address
City, State   Zip Code

_____
Staff Representative

_____
University Officer

187

Appendix L

INVESTMENT COMMITMENT IN
THE _____ COLLEGE OR UNIVERSITY

In consideration of my interest in education and for and in consideration of the similar promises of other donors, and to induce others to contribute to _____ College/University and in consideration of the University's promise to use this gift as specified herein and the University's actions in reliance on this pledge, and other good and valuable consideration, the receipt of which is hereby acknowledged, and intending to be legally bound hereby, I/we hereby pledge and promise to pay to_____ College/University the sum of $_____.

This gift will be used for_____

_____and this promise to use and the use by the University of the amount pledged shall in itself constitute full and adequate consideration for this pledge.

This commitment will be paid to THE PENNSYLVANIA STATE UNIVERSITY in the following manner:

PLEDGE YEAR 1 $_____

PLEDGE YEAR 2 $_____

PLEDGE YEAR 3 $_____

PLEDGE YEAR 4 $_____

PLEDGE YEAR 5 $_____

_____ Total amount for this year's gift is enclosed.
_____ I/We prefer to make the annual gifts in the month of _____, beginning 19___.

I/We prefer to make this gift in the following manner:

_____ Cash Securities, or Real Property   _____ Charitable Trust
_____ Life Insurance   _____ Gift Annuity
_____ Pooled Income Fund   _____ Other (please specify)
                                                _____

_____ Additional funds will be forthcoming through matching gifts from my company or my spouse's company which is

_____
Company Name

This pledge is to be irrevocable and a binding obligation upon me, my estate, my executors and my heirs. This pledge shall be governed and interpreted under the laws of the Commonwealth of Pennsylvania. In witness whereof, I/we hereby sign and seal this Pledge Agreement with the intention to be legally bound hereby.

_____   _____
Signature   Date

_____   _____
Signature   Date

Please acknowledge and credit this gift in the following way:

_____
Name(s) (please print)

_____
Street

_____
City, State, Zip Code

                                        Pledge Accepted By:
                                        Office of University Development
Please make checks payable to: _____ COLLEGE OR UNIVERSITY
_____ College or University   Street Address
                                        City, State   Zip Code

                                        _____
THE PLEDGE YEAR runs from   Staff Representative
July 1 through June 30.
LBP   _____
                                        University Officer

189

Appendix

Appendix M

CASE CAMPAIGN STANDARDS

MANAGEMENT AND REPORTING STANDARDS FOR EDUCATIONAL FUND-RAISING CAMPAIGNS

. . . .

Endorsed by

American Association of Colleges of Nursing (AACN)
American Association of Community Colleges (AACC)
American Association of Fund-Raising Counsel (AAFRC)
American Council on Education (ACE)
American Prospect Research Association (APRA)
Association of Community College Trustees (ACCT)
Association of Healthcare Philanthropy
Canadian Council of Advancement Executives (CCAE)
The College Board
Council of Graduate Schools (CGS)
Council of Independent Colleges (CIC)
Lilly Endowment, Inc.
National Association of College and University Business Officers (NACUBO)
National Association of Independent Colleges and Universities (NAICU)
National Association of Independent Schools (NAIS)
National Association of State Universities and Land-Grant Colleges (NASULGC)
National Council for Resource Development (NCRD)
National University Continuing Education Association (NUCEA)

COUNCIL FOR ADVANCEMENT AND SUPPORT OF EDUCATION
Approved by the CASE Board of Trustees, April 18, 1994

Table of Contents

Statements from AGB and NACUBO:

" The Board of Directors of the Association of Governing Boards of Universities and Colleges (AGB) commends CASE for developing the *CASE Campaign Standards*. AGB endorses the standards except for those provisions addressing testamentary bequests and deferred gifts. AGB urges institutions to count bequests only when actually realized. With regard to deferred gifts, AGB urges that campaign totals be based on present value only."

"The National Association of College and University Business Officers (NACUBO) endorses the management and non-financial reporting standards developed by CASE that are presented in this publication. Application of these standards by colleges and universities will contribute to an industry-wide improvement in the accurate determination and interpretation of fund-raising information.

Institutions should be mindful that the standards regarding reporting of testamentary pledges differ from generally accepted accounting practices and hence will lead to reporting differences between these management reports and general purpose financial statements of the institution."

All inquiries should be directed to the
Council for Advancement and Support of Education
Suite 400, 11 Dupont Circle, Washington, DC 20036-1261
Telephone: (202) 328-5900   Fax: (202) 387-4973
Internet: *efr@ns.case.org*

i

Foreword

The document you are reading is the culmination of a major effort by the educational community to bring a higher standard of conduct to one of the most visible activities in the academy: the fund-raising campaign. The officers and trustees of the Council for Advancement and Support of Education (CASE) urge all institutions that are planning or conducting campaigns to adopt these standards. They go into effect for the academic year beginning July 1, 1994, with reports on the fiscal 1994-95 results due to CASE in December 1995.

This document represents four years of intensive effort by a small group of volunteer and staff professionals who worked tirelessly to reach consensus on a complex undertaking. The Campaign Reporting Advisory Group prepared numerous drafts and distributed them for comment to CASE members, selected committees of the National Association of College and University Business Officers, members of the American Association of Fund-Raising Counsel, educational representatives on the board of the National Committee on Planned Giving, and many other parties. The advisory committee also considered the scores of comments they received, debated the issues, and ultimately came to the conclusions in this document.

For their selfless commitment of time and expertise, I want to express CASE's deep thanks to all the members of the Campaign Reporting Advisory Group, whose names appear on the next page.

But two people deserve special credit: Dr. Vance T. Peterson, chair of the advisory group and vice president for institutional advancement at Occidental College; and Mary Joan McCarthy, vice president for administration of the professional services group at CASE. Although universal voluntary compliance will ultimately be the measure of these standards' effectiveness, we owe these two professionals enormous gratitude for their work in bringing them about.

To encourage all educational institutions in the United States and Canada to comply with these standards, I have asked associations in both countries to endorse them. I am pleased that several leading corporations and foundations have also indicated interest in supporting them. CASE is grateful to Lilly Endowment, Inc. for its endorsement and for funding the printing and distribution of *CASE Campaign Standards*.

So that professionals will understand and use the standards, CASE will include training sessions about them at many of its educational fund-raising conferences and at its eight North American district conferences in 1994 and 1995. Also, to encourage consistency among reporting standards, CASE will begin to revise the gift reporting section of the 1982 document *Management Reporting Standards for Educational Institutions: Fund Raising and Related Activities*. When that revision is complete, CASE plans to combine into one publication the two standards documents.

All of us who have contributed to these standards hope and expect that they will strengthen education and the philanthropic spirit that undergirds it, for the future benefit of society.

Peter McE. Buchanan
President, Council for Advancement
and Support of Education

ii

Campaign Reporting Advisory Group

Vance T. Peterson, Ph.D., Chair
Vice President, Institutional Advancement
Occidental College

G. David Gearhart
Senior Vice President for
 Development and University Relations
The Pennsylvania State University

Martin Grenzebach
Chairman
John Grenzebach & Associates, Inc.

Warren Heemann
Vice President for Development
 and Alumni Relations
University of Chicago

James A. Hyatt
Associate Chancellor for
 Budget and Planning
University of California, Berkeley

Roy E. Muir
Associate Vice President for Development
University of Michigan

James F. Ridenour
Senior Consultant
Marts & Lundy, Inc.

STAFF

Richard A. Edwards
Senior Vice President
 Professional Services Group
CASE

Mary Joan McCarthy
Vice President for Administration
 Professional Services Group
CASE

Why Institutions Need Campaign Standards

*T*he capital or comprehensive fundraising campaign is a vehicle for focusing attention upon the needs and aspirations of an educational community. A campaign is thus an important event in the life of any institution striving for greater financial stability and excellence.

The recent trend toward campaigns that raise hundreds of millions or even billions of dollars has boosted the visibility of fund raising in general and the role of campaigns in particular. This visibility has also heightened the pressure on fund raisers and financial managers to ensure their campaigns' success.

At the same time, and in part because of their sheer size, campaigns are being scrutinized with growing intensity by faculties, governing bodies, donors, and beneficiaries. Together with the public at large they want, and deserve, to know exactly what impact such campaigns will have on their institutions.

It is, therefore, of vital importance that institutions have two measures for their work: first, an objective means to compare one campaign to another, and second, a rational way to discern how well any given campaign has met the goals that spurred the institution to conduct the campaign in the first place.

This document is designed to address these two issues. Its goal is to establish guidance for managing campaigns and standards for reporting campaign gifts in the United States and Canada. Such standards should help avoid invidious comparisons among campaigns of different types and purposes. They should also help institutions articulate the impact of any given campaign to various constituencies.

These standards depend upon three fundamental concepts:

(1) campaign reports should separate results by (a) the campaign's featured objectives[1] and (b) the campaign's other objectives;

(2) campaign reports should separate outright/current gifts and pledges from deferred gifts the institution expects to receive after the solicitation and pledge-payment periods end; and

(3) the reports should record these deferred gifts at both their face value and their discounted present value. If bequest expectancies or the death benefit of life insurance are counted, they should be treated in the same way.

All of these measures are important to helping faculty, volunteers, donors, institutional administrators, and the general public reach a common understanding of the true impact of campaign fund raising.

These standards are rooted in two important convictions. One is that how well the campaign meets its objectives is far more important than the size of its dollar goal. The other is that success should be measured primarily in terms of how well the institution meets its own needs and fulfills its unique mission. Working from these convictions, the many people who helped create these standards have a lofty ambition for what the standards will ultimately achieve.

---

[1] Every campaign is designed to help meet specific institutional needs. While all educational institutions have many ongoing needs for outside funding, those specifically featured in the campaign priorities list or case statement are considered "featured objectives."

They, and the Council for Advancement and Support of Education, believe that by setting high standards for conducting campaigns and reporting their results, philanthropy will be strengthened and protected, and public confidence in education will be enhanced.

CASE Campaign Standards is intended as a supplement to *Management Reporting Standards for Educational Institutions: Fund Raising and Related Activities* (CASE/NACUBO, 1982). Each educational institution conducting a campaign is asked to file a report annually with CASE.

The report to CASE consists of Appendices A and B, which are included on pages 13-15 in this document. CASE will organize and publish the information from these reports annually as a service to its membership and the public at large. The CASE report will provide fund-raising professionals, consultants, educational leaders, and volunteers with a common language for discussing their campaigns and comparing them from institution to institution.

Appendix A consists of a questionnaire about the institution and its campaign. Appendix B: Campaign Report I is a form for reporting a campaign's financial results in three primary columns plus two columns for totals:

(1) current gifts and pledges reported at face value;

(2) deferred gifts (future commitments) reported at face value for featured objectives and other objectives;

(3) deferred gifts (future commitments) reported at the gift's discounted present value for featured objectives and other objectives;

(4) the sum of 1 and 2 above; and

(5) the sum of 1 and 3 above.

This multi-column reporting approach is the result of lengthy discussions with CASE members about the pros and cons of reporting deferred gifts (future commitments) at present value versus face value. While discounting to present value represents a substantial change from past practice, many people strongly support its use as a more realistic indicator of the future value those dollars will have when the institution actually is able to spend them. Also, this method accounts for any pay-out obligations to the donor.

At the same time, this approach recognizes the concern about the potential negative impact present-value discounting could have on donors. When donors make an irrevocable deferred gift, they turn over an asset to the institution and give up their control of it. And, even though the institution may pay back a substantial amount to the donor and will not be able to spend the asset for some time into the future, many donors consider the current face value of the asset as the amount that he or she gave to the institution.

Therefore, the standards create three primary reporting columns, plus two columns for totals, to accommodate these concerns. Those who believe that publicly displaying the present value of deferred gifts will, in fact, discourage donors from making such gifts may choose to report only the first two columns to their constituents, but those institutions should report *all* columns on Appendix B to their appropriate governing boards and to CASE. CASE will in turn report *all* columns in its published report of campaign results. These standards are, therefore, silent on the question of how an institution should publicly recognize its donors.

Vance T. Peterson
Chair, Campaign Reporting Advisory Group
Vice President, Institutional Advancement,
  Occidental College

Chapter I 1

Guidelines for Campaign Management

*F*und-raising campaigns for educational institutions, often referred to as capital campaigns, are a means by which institutions intensify for a finite period their continuing efforts to raise money. They have evolved from campaigns that most often sought cash over a period of a year or two for a single capital objective, such as the construction of a building, into complex undertakings. Today, campaigns may run for seven years or more and may seek both cash and intricate deferred gifts for current operations and a variety of capital purposes (including building construction, renovation, and endowments). Whereas once campaigns usually served single, readily understood purposes and had goals in the tens of millions of dollars, they now are often organized as responses to the needs of entire campuses, and success is measured in the hundreds of millions, even billions of dollars.

The scope of today's campaigns, their complexity, the sophisticated knowledge required to understand them, and their promotional nature together can create misunderstanding about the purposes of campaigns and what they will achieve. When the critical needs of an institution are identified, a goal is set that would fund them, and the goal is attained, the faculty, administration, and volunteers assume the institution's problems are solved. Too often this is not the case, leaving members of the academic community and the general public confused and dissatisfied.

The following recommendations are offered to help alleviate these concerns.

CAMPAIGN DESIGN

Care should be taken to design campaigns that reconcile the needs of the institution with the interest and capacity of its constituencies to fund them. The strength of the development program, including the size of the investment that has and will be made in it throughout the campaign, must also be factored into the design. The tendency of institutions to focus their attention on the size of the goal of their proposed campaign rather than what should and can realistically be achieved is probably the greatest cause of dissatisfaction with campaign results. When the desire to have a large goal influences an institution's decision regarding campaign objectives, the length of the advance-gifts phase (also known as the nucleus fund), the duration of the public phase, and the accounting policies it adopts, that campaign will tend to favor public relations over academic purpose.

CAMPAIGN PLAN

A written plan should be prepared and reviewed by all appropriate bodies of the institution. This document should describe, at a minimum:

(1) the institution's financial needs that will be addressed;

(2) the campaign reporting policies to which the institution will adhere (including the treatment of pledges, deferred gifts, and gifts-in-kind);

(3) the manner in which exceptions to those policies will be considered and acted upon;

2

(4) the tentative goal for both featured objectives (usually endowment and construction) and other objectives (usually expendable programmatic support and annual fund revenues);

(5) an objective analysis of the fund-raising potential of the institution;

(6) the purpose and duration of the advance-gifts phase of the campaign; and

(7) the duration of the public phase of the campaign.

The plan should be approved formally by the committee organized to assist in the planning of the campaign and the appropriate governing board of the institution. It also should be reviewed and commented upon by all other interested bodies of the institution.

It follows that the advance-gifts phase of a campaign cannot begin until the campaign plan is approved and that the institution should not reach back and credit to its campaign gifts that were received prior to the plan's endorsement.

CAMPAIGN PURPOSES

Those planning campaigns are encouraged to keep in mind that campaigns can achieve several purposes and should design their campaigns with all those purposes in mind. These include the articulation and dissemination of: the case for support of the institution; the defining of its priority needs; the nurturing of the development program and staff; the broadening and deepening of volunteer participation; and the strengthening of the working relationship among the institution's volunteer leadership, including its governing board, faculty, students, administration, alumni, and friends.

They should also keep in mind that no campaign will be the last campaign, and care must be taken to conduct it in a way that will serve the institution's long-term best interests. Neither the needs of the institution nor the results achieved by the campaign's success should be exaggerated. It should be made clear that high participation—by young as well as more mature alumni, by persons of modest means as well as the wealthy—will be an important factor in gauging the campaign's success. The gratitude of the institution and those volunteers working on its behalf should be communicated promptly and graciously to all who have made gifts. All volunteers should be kept informed of the campaign's progress in a systematic way and recognized publicly for the important role they played in the campaign.

Finally, when planning a campaign, consideration should be given to the work that needs to be done following its formal conclusion. Volunteers need to be thanked, pledges collected, and reports made and distributed. And most important, serious and imaginative thought must be given to ways in which the valuable relationships established in the course of the campaign will be not only maintained but nurtured and strengthened during the years that follow.

CAMPAIGN MARKETING

Campaign marketing should be proportional to institutional requirements. While campaign case statements and other literature or presentations should be designed to inspire and motivate donors, such materials should not be used to distort institutional accomplishments, characteristics, or capabilities. Campaign managers also are cautioned to balance the marketing of outright and deferred support in their presentations. Both types of gifts play an important role in campaigns, and both should be given visibility in a well-rounded campaign.

CAMPAIGN RECOGNITION

Special care should be taken by campaign managers to devise appropriate ways of recognizing all contributors during a capital campaign (keeping in mind Internal Revenue Service regulations on premiums) even if their gifts may fall technically outside of what is appropriately counted according to these standards. For example, while most institutions currently choose not to include testamentary pledges of any type in their campaign totals, the individuals responsible for making such commitments during the campaign still should be recognized in some fashion for having responded to the institution's request for increased support. Most institutions recognize testamentary commitments through a special recognition society of some type.

Campaign Reporting Standards

CAMPAIGN PERIOD

For purposes of these standards, the "Campaign Period" refers to the total time encompassed by the active solicitation period for the campaign, including the advance-gifts phase. CASE recommends that no campaign period exceed seven years in duration. Generally speaking, shorter campaign periods are preferable to longer ones.

PLEDGE-PAYMENT PERIOD

The pledge-payment period should not exceed five years.

FUNDAMENTAL PRINCIPLES OF CAMPAIGN COUNTING

The following basic principles for counting campaign gifts are applicable to all institutions and all types of campaigns:

(1) only those gifts and pledges actually received or committed during the specific period of time identified for the campaign (a period up to seven years including the advance-gifts phase) should be counted in campaign totals;

(2) the advance-gifts phase of a campaign is always a part of the designated campaign period, and commitments reported for this phase must actually have been received or pledged during this specified period within the campaign time frame;

(3) gifts and pledges may be counted to only one campaign; and

(4) the value of any cancelled or unfulfilled pledges must be subtracted from campaign totals when it is determined they will not be realized.

ADVANCE-GIFTS PHASE/ NUCLEUS-FUND PHASE

The advance-gifts or nucleus-fund phase is that period of time prior to public announcement of the campaign, or the campaign's official goal, during which pace-setting gifts are sought from individuals and organizations closest to the institution. As indicated above, the advance-gifts phase should be considered a part of the campaign period.

Defining the advance-gifts phase as part of the campaign period will also help ensure that so-called "reach back" gifts are not counted.

It is preferable that credit for gifts received in the advance-gifts phase of a campaign be limited to those gifts given for featured objectives, thereby strengthening the focus of campaign efforts and eventual results. Another approach is to have a comprehensive advance-gifts phase, during which *all* gifts and pledges are counted. If this approach is adopted, it is critical that campaign managers explain to institutional personnel and campaign volunteers that reported results will inflate somewhat the true impact of the campaign effort.

Whichever method is used, the key principles at work are:

(1) the advance-gifts period should be limited to a set number of months or years, and

(2) this period of time should be included as part of the total campaign duration.

WHAT TO REPORT

All gifts and pledges falling into categories covered by these standards may be reported. The spirit of these standards, however, is that it is never appropriate to report only one number when announcing campaign results. As a minimum, the following results should be reported to the institution's board and in the report to CASE:

(1) *the total of outright gifts and pledges received, reported at face value,* and payable within the campaign period and post-campaign accounting period as specified in the campaign plan;

(2) *the total of deferred (future) commitments, reported at face value,* which will be received at an undetermined time in the future;

(3) *the total of deferred (future) commitments, discounted to present value,* which will be received at an undetermined time in the future;

(4) the grand total of 1 and 2 above; and

(5) the grand total of 1 and 3 above.

Additionally, totals for the campaign's featured objectives vs. other campaign objectives would be appropriate in most campaign reporting.

As noted in the preface, institutions that believe publicly displaying the present value of deferred gifts will in fact discourage their donors from making such gifts may choose to report only the first two columns to their constituents, but should report *all* columns from Appendix B to their boards and in their reports to CASE.

Both campaign staff and counsel should take pains to ensure that campaign publicity clearly states the results of the campaign in accordance with these categorical standards.

WHEN TO REPORT GIFTS

Outright gifts should be reported only when assets are transferred irrevocably to the institution or an institutionally related foundation. Deferred gifts should be reported only when assets are transferred or, in cases where no assets are transferred, when a legally binding deferred pledge agreement or other irrevocable document is consummated with the institution.

HOW TO REPORT GIFTS

Appendices B and C are viewed as basic tools of reporting campaign activity. Appendix B: "Campaign Report I" summarizes results by campaign objectives and sources, further separates gifts and pledges to be received during the campaign solicitation period or the immediate post-campaign accounting period from commitments of funds to be received at some indeterminate time in the future, and records deferred gifts at both face value *and* present value.

Appendix C: "Campaign Report II" summarizes gifts, pledges, and deferred gift arrangements by type, according to when they will be received by the institution. This "cash flow" projection report is important to institutional budget planners and others interested in understanding the immediate and future impact of a campaign on the institution.

PLEDGES

(1) *Oral Pledges:* Oral pledges should not be reported in campaign totals. On the rare occasion when special circumstances may

6

warrant making an exception, the advancement officer should write to the individual making an oral pledge to document the commitment, place a copy of the written commitment in the donor's file, and gain specific written approval from a gift acceptance committee made up of institutional and volunteer representatives.

(2) *Pledges of Cash:* Pledges of cash should be written and should commit to a specific dollar amount that will be paid according to a fixed time schedule. The pledge payment period, regardless of when the pledge is made, should not exceed five years. Therefore, a pledge received even on the last day of the campaign is counted in campaign totals and may be paid over a five-year period.

(3) *Testamentary Pledges and Deferred Pledge Agreements* (see Appendices F and G).

EXCLUSIONS

The following types of funds should be excluded from campaign report totals:

(1) gifts or pledges, outright and deferred, that already have been counted in previous campaigns, even if realized during the campaign-reporting period;

(2) investment earnings on gifts, even if accrued during the campaign-reporting period and even if required within the terms specified by a donor (the only exception permitted to this exclusion would be in-terest accumulations counted in guaranteed investment instruments that mature within the time frame of the campaign, such as zero coupon bonds);

(3) earned income, including transfer payments from medical or analogous practice plans;

(4) surplus income transfers from ticket-based operations, except for any amount equal to that permitted as a charitable deduction by the IRS/Revenue Canada;

(5) contract revenues;

(6) contributed services, except for those permitted as a charitable deduction by IRS/Revenue Canada; and

(7) governmental funds. It is recognized that certain state and federal government programs requiring private matching funds bear a special relationship to the encouragement of philanthropy. Nevertheless, the difference between public and private support is profound within the American tradition.

Campaigns are clearly instruments of philanthropy while governments are channels for the implementation of public policy. While both philanthropy and public policy may be motivated by compassion for others, only philanthropy involves the disposition of privately held resources for the public good. *Governmental funds should NOT be reported in campaign totals.*

Chapter III   7

Standards for Reporting Certain Types Of Gifts and Pledges

CASH

Report cash at full value as of the date received by the institution.

MARKETABLE SECURITIES

Marketable securities should be counted at the average of the high and low quoted selling prices (or the average of the bid/ask in the case of certain securities) on the date the donor relinquished dominion and control of the assets in favor of the institution or trust. Exactly when dominion and control has been relinquished by a donor depends upon the method of delivery of the securities to the donee. These reporting standards do not address the multitude of tax rules regarding the delivery of securities by the donor to the donee.

CLOSELY HELD STOCK

Gifts of closely held stock exceeding $10,000 in value should be reported at the fair market value placed on them by a qualified independent appraiser as required by the IRS[2] for valuing gifts of nonpublicly traded stock. Gifts of $10,000 or less may be valued at the per-share cash purchase price of the most recent transaction. Normally, this transaction will be the redemption of the stock by the corporation.

If no redemption is consummated during the campaign period, a gift of closely held stock may be credited to campaign totals at the value determined by a qualified independent appraiser. For a gift of $10,000 or less, when no redemption has occurred during the campaign period, an independent CPA who maintains the books for a

closely held corporation is deemed to be qualified to value the stock of the corporation.

GIFTS OF PROPERTY

Gifts of real and personal property for which donors qualify for a charitable deduction should be counted at their full fair-market value. Gifts in kind, such as equipment and software, shall be counted at their educational discount value, which, for purposes of these standards of reporting, shall be deemed to be fair-market value.

Caution should be exercised to ensure that only gifts that are convertible to cash or that are of actual value to the institution are included in campaign totals. Gifts with fair-market values exceeding $5,000 should be counted at the values placed on them by qualified independent appraisers as required by the IRS for valuing noncash charitable contributions. Gifts of $5,000 and under may be reported at the value declared by the donor or placed on them by a qualified expert on the faculty or staff of the institution.

CHARITABLE REMAINDER TRUSTS AND POOLED INCOME FUNDS

Gifts made to establish charitable remainder trusts (including charitable remainder trusts administered outside the institution) where the remainder is not subject to change or revocation, and contributions to pooled income funds should be credited to the "future commitments" section of campaign totals at both the discounted present value of the remainder interest allowable as a deduction by the *Internal Revenue Code* (see

---

[2] Contact the IRS/Revenue Canada for its specific definition of qualified independent appraiser.

Appendix B, Column III) and at face value (see Column II).

The premise underlying the discounting to present value of gifts of a future interest is that the present value of a future interest is less than the current value. See Appendix D for a discussion of present value of gifts. For Canadian institutions, the discounted present value for reporting should be that value calculated by the institution's accountant, actuary, or by software capable of producing present value calculations.

Note: Recognizing that the details of all charitable remainder trust gifts may not be available to the institution, and thus verification that they are irrevocable will not always be possible, the Campaign Reporting Advisory Group nonetheless believes strongly that the trust must be irrevocable in order to be counted in campaign totals.

CHARITABLE GIFT ANNUITIES

Gifts made in exchange for an annuity are technically outright gifts subject to a condition that the donee pay an annuity for life or lives of one or more annuitants. Thus, there is no "remainder interest." However, because the donee receives less than the entire amount transferred—only the excess of the gifted value over the cost to the donee of producing the annuity—gift annuities should be reported in the same two sections as gifts of charitable remainder trusts and pooled-income funds.

The face amount transferred should be reported in Appendix B, Column II, and the amount allowable as a deduction under the *Internal Revenue Code* (the face value minus the present value of the annuity) should be reported in Column III along with present values of remainders. This reporting will also reflect both state and province laws requiring the maintenance of reserves against the annuity payments to be made and, in those without mandated reserves, the generally accepted accounting practices that also suggest the maintenance of such reserves.

Reserve requirements and accounting practice reserve amounts vary widely; this method of reporting will provide consistency of campaign reporting from all states and provinces.

REMAINDER INTEREST IN A RESIDENCE OR FARM

A gift of a remainder interest in a personal residence or farm should be credited in the "future commitments" section of campaign totals at both the remainder value recognized as an allowable deduction by the IRS and at the face value.

CHARITABLE LEAD TRUSTS

Because charitable lead trusts are not deferred gifts, but are immediate gifts in trust that pay over a period of time, the calculation of face and present values is slightly different than for a charitable remainder trust or a pooled-income fund. For lead trusts whose terms extend five years or less, the face value as described in this section may be reported under the current "gifts and pledges" section of campaign totals.

For charitable lead trusts that extend beyond five years, the institution should report amounts beyond the first five-year "gift and pledges" value both at *remaining* face value of the income stream in Column II and at discounted present value of the *remaining* income stream.

For this purpose, face value of the charitable lead annuity trust is the aggregate of annuity dollars to be received by the institution for the term of the charitable lead annuity trust. *Remaining* face value is the aggregate of annuity dollars to be received for all years beyond the first five-year pledge period.

The face value of the lead unitrust is more difficult to ascertain because the trust value for each year of the trust term is an unknown, thus the total amount to be received by the institution is also unknown. A credible estimate of the total income to be received from a charitable lead unitrust should be made using as the trust's earnings the Applicable Federal Rate (AFR) for the month in which the trust was funded. Use of the AFR for estimating lead unitrust earnings (and therefore trust values) is consistent with reporting for remainder trusts and will obviate arbitrary selection of assumed earnings rates among institutions.

Thus, the trust's yearly values will be deemed to grow or shrink over the years of the trust term depending on the relationship of the trust to the institution as compared to the AFR. Then, based on trust values, trust payouts to the institution can be estimated. The aggregate of payouts is, for this purpose, the face value. *Remaining* face value is the total amount to be received for all years beyond the first five-year pledge period. This latter amount is reported in Column II.

Discounted present value for both types of lead trusts should be the amount allowable as a deduction (for either income or gift/estate tax purposes). To calculate the *remaining* discounted present value for the trust term beyond the five-year pledge reporting period, use the present value of the full-trust term minus the present value of the five-year term.

This will require two separate present value calculations, one for the full-trust term and the other as if the lead trust were to run only for five years. Subtract the five-year discounted value from the discounted value of the full term to find the *remaining* discounted value of the trust term beyond the five-year pledge period. This *remaining* present value is reported in Column III.

Any of the deduction calculation software programs on the market is capable of performing these calculations.

WHOLLY CHARITABLE TRUSTS ADMINISTERED BY OTHERS

A wholly charitable trust is one that is held for the benefit of charity, where the principal is invested and the income is distributed to charitable organizations. All interests in income and principal are irrevocably dedicated to charitable purposes (as opposed to a charitable remainder or lead trust). While it is similar in that sense to an endowment fund, it is created as a free-standing entity.

The fair-market value of the assets, or a portion of the assets, of such a trust administered by an outside fiduciary should be counted in the "gifts and pledges" section of campaign totals for the year in which the trust is established, *provided* that the institution has an irrevocable right to all or a predetermined portion of the income of the trust.

The amount to be reported in the case where less than the entire income of the trust is to be distributed to the institution is the amount of the income to be distributed to the institution over the total income (or the stated percentage to be distributed, if the trust terms spell this out as a percentage) multiplied by the value of the trust assets. The income of the trust is thereafter treated as endowment income and does not appear in the amounts reported under gifts.

NON-GOVERNMENT GRANTS AND CONTRACTS

Grant income from private, non-government sources should be reported; *contract revenue should be excluded.* The difference between a private grant and contract should be judged on the basis of the intention of the awarding agency and the legal obligation incurred by an institution in accepting the award. A grant, like a gift, is bestowed voluntarily and without expectation of any

10

tangible compensation. It is donative in nature. A contract carries an explicit "quid pro quo" relationship between the source and the institution.

TESTAMENTARY PLEDGE COMMITMENTS

The decision to include or exclude testamentary pledges in campaign totals is left up to each institution. For some institutions and for certain types of donors and circumstances, the counting of testamentary pledge commitments may be appropriate. For others, depending on institutional history and campaign objectives, the practice would not be acceptable. *If* the decision is made to include testamentary commitments in campaign totals, however, the following standards for handling such commitments should be followed.

Institutions choosing to include testamentary pledge commitments in campaign totals should satisfy the following three requirements:

(1) credit commitments that have a specified amount or percentage of the estate stated in the will based on a credible estimate of the future value of the estate at the time the commitment is made;

Note: Fund-raising practitioners will appreciate that there is no single or simple way to estimate the future value of an estate commitment. For this reason many institutions have chosen to exclude testamentary pledges entirely from campaign totals. Nevertheless, others feel that testamentary gifts should be included in campaign reports, especially since these often are part of a total campaign commitment being made by a donor. The key to making the decision about whether or not these types of gifts should be given campaign credit is often the determination of future value of the estate. At best, this requires a judgment call to be made by the institution after conversation with the donor and his/her adviser.

(2) have verification of the commitment in *one* of the following forms:

(a) a letter from the donor or the donor's attorney affirming the commitment and stating that the institution will be informed of any changes in the will that might be made in the future; *or,*

(b) bearing in mind that in some states the following options have not been legally affirmed, the commitment could be accompanied either by a deferred-pledge agreement or a contract to make a will (see below and Appendices F and G)[3]:

Charitable/Deferred-pledge Agreement. A deferred-pledge agreement is a legally binding document tested in the courts of several states that places an obligation on the estate of the issuer to transfer a certain amount to the institution. Under such agreements, the executor of the donor's estate is held legally responsible for payment of the specified amount from the estate (see Appendix F for sample).

Contract to Make a Will. A contract to make a will is a legally binding document, also tested in the courts of several states, that places an obligation on the donor to make a will that transfers certain assets or a certain percentage of his or her estate to the institution. This instrument is used when the donor cannot (or does not wish to) specify the precise dollar amount he or she will contribute. Instead, the donor promises to execute a valid will wherein he or she designates a certain item of property or a portion of his or her estate to the institution.

---

[3] Specific legal instruments vary from state to state.

Often, this portion is stated as a percentage of the residue of the estate. After the contract is signed, no changes may be made in the donor's will that would decrease the institution's originally specified share, except as agreed upon in advance by the donor and the institution (see Appendix G for sample); and

(3) the amount specified or estimated should be reported at both the discounted present value and at face value in the deferred/future commitments portion of campaign reports (see Appendix D).

Further, institutions choosing to report testamentary pledge commitments are strongly urged to investigate carefully the actual circumstances underlying the estate and err on the side of conservatism in counting such commitments toward campaign totals. *If any circumstances should make it unlikely that the amount pledged by bequest will actually be realized by the institution, then the commitment should be further adjusted according to specific circumstances, or not reported at all.*

REALIZED TESTAMENTARY GIFTS

All bequests realized during the defined duration of the campaign should be counted at full value in campaign totals so long as no gift amount was counted in a previous campaign.

LIFE INSURANCE

Institutions may or may not wish to include commitments of life insurance in campaign totals. *If* gifts of life insurance are to be included, the institution should be made the owner and irrevocable beneficiary of the policies, with the exception of realized death benefits.

(1) *Paid-up Life Insurance Policies.* Paid-up life insurance policies may be counted in one of two ways:

(a) the cash surrender value, counted as a current outright gift (Column I); or

(b) the death benefit value, counted at both the face value and the discounted present value (Columns II and III).

Each institution should decide, in advance of its campaign, which of the two methods will be used to count gifts of paid-up life insurance policies and then use that method exclusively for the duration of the campaign.

Cautionary note: Caution should be exercised in valuing such commitments for the "future commitments" section of campaign totals, because life insurance policies may not actually be worth the full stated value of the insured amount.

For example, the cash value may have been borrowed against or the insurance company itself may have invaded cash value to meet missed premium payments. In such cases, loans would have to be repaid from any death benefit proceeds due to the beneficiary. Certain policies may also contain a provision wherein the insured amount is decreased significantly after a certain age has been attained. In all such cases, the *lesser* amount should be used to calculate the present value to be credited to the campaign.

(2) *Existing Policies/Not Fully Paid Up.* A life insurance policy that is not fully paid up on the date of contribution, which is given to the institution during the period of the campaign, should be counted at the existing cash value in the gifts and pledges section, Column I, in campaign totals. In addition, where the payment of premiums is pledged over a five-year pledge period, the incremental increase of the cash value should be counted in the gifts and pledges section, Column I.

(3) *New Policies.* The cash surrender value of premiums paid (or pledged over a five-year period) on policies for which donors apply and contribute to the institution during the period of the campaign should be counted in the current gifts and pledges section in campaign totals.

(4) *Realized Death Benefits.* The insurance company's settlement amount for an insurance policy whose death benefit is realized during the campaign period, whether the policy is owned by the institution or not, should be counted in campaign totals, provided no gift amount was counted in a previous campaign.

SPECIAL CIRCUMSTANCES

If a deferred gift by bequest, life insurance, trust, or gift annuity has been counted for the campaign as a future commitment in Columns II and III and the life income recipient (for gift annuities, pooled-income funds, and charitable remainder trusts), the insured (on a life insurance policy), or the testator (of a bequest) dies within a five-year reporting period for the campaign, resulting in the institution, receiving the gift in full, the institution may revise its crediting of the gift to reflect that the gift is fully paid during the allowable five-year period by deleting it from "future commitments" Columns II and III and replacing the full value in "current gifts and pledges" Column I. This is to reflect consistency in reporting these receipts with gifts and pledges paid during a five-year reporting period.

With special thanks, CASE and the Campaign Reporting Advisory Group acknowledge Lynda S. Moerschbaecher's technical and writing contributions to this chapter.

CASE Voluntary Annual Survey of Cumulative Campaign Activity by Member Institutions

This is a sample of the form CASE will ask institutions that are planning a campaign or are in a campaign to complete and submit to CASE annually. CASE will keep information on campaigns not yet publicly announced confidential.

Campaign results as of June 30, 19____, representing year ____ of the campaign period.

A. CAMPAIGN GOAL: $ _____

Current Operations $ _____
Capital Projects $ _____
Endowment $ _____

B. CAMPAIGN GOAL:

Outright $ _____
Deferred $ _____

C. PROGRESS TOWARD GOAL: *(to date)*

Column IV from Appendix B $ _____

Column V from Appendix B $ _____

D. EXTERNAL REPORTS TO DONORS:

Check which reports from Appendix B are used in External Reports to donors:

____ Columns I & II
____ Columns I & III
____ Both

E. INSTITUTIONAL DATA:

Alumni of record _____
E&G Budget _____
FTE Students _____

F. CAMPAIGN SCOPE: *(check one)*

____ Single unit—school, center, etc.
____ Several units—but not all
____ Comprehensive—total institution

G. LENGTH OF CAMPAIGN PERIOD:
(check one)

____ 1 Year   ____ 5 Years
____ 2 Years   ____ 6 Years
____ 3 Years   ____ 7 Years
____ 4 Years

H. DO CAMPAIGN TOTALS INCLUDE TESTAMENTARY COMMITMENTS?

____ Yes ____ No

If yes, are CASE standards met?
____ Yes ____ No *(please explain)*

_____
_____
_____

I. DO CAMPAIGN TOTALS INCLUDE LIFE INSURANCE?

____ Yes ____ No

If yes, by what method of counting?
____ Cash-surrender value only
____ Face value/present value
____ Realized death benefit only

14

J. MAXIMUM PLEDGE PAYMENT PERIOD:

_____ 3 Years

_____ 4 Years

_____ 5 Years

_____ Other *(please explain)*

_____

_____

_____

K. ADVANCE-GIFTS (NUCLEUS-FUND) PHASE INCLUDES IN TOTALS:

_____ Gifts to featured objectives only

_____ All gifts received by the institution

L. FOR THE REPORTING YEAR, IN WHAT PHASE WAS YOUR INSTITUTION'S CAMPAIGN?

_____ Pre-campaign planning

_____ Advance gifts/nucleus fund

_____ General public phase

_____ Post-campaign accounting

M. PLEASE ENTER DATES FOR THE FOLLOWING: *(month/year)*

_____ Began crediting gifts

_____ Campaign was publicly announced

_____ Campaign will be publicly announced

_____ Completion or targeted completion

Institution: _____

Address: _____

Submitted by: _____

Title: _____

Telephone: _____ Fax: _____

CERTIFICATION OF COMPLIANCE

(fill in name of institution and sign)

Please complete the appropriate sentence below:

1. _____ adheres fully to *CASE Campaign Standards*.

2. _____ adheres generally to the *CASE Campaign Standards* but with the following specific exception(s) *(please use additional paper if necessary)*:

_____

_____

_____

_____

Name of Chief Executive Officer (please print)

Signature of Chief Executive Officer   Date

Campaign Report I: Results by Objective and Source

This is a sample of the report CASE will ask institutions that are in a campaign to complete and submit to CASE with Appendix A.

	Column I CURRENT/OUTRIGHT *GIFTS AND PLEDGES*[1] (FACE VALUE)		Column II DEFERRED GIFTS *Future Commitments*[2] (FACE VALUE)		Column III DEFERRED GIFTS *Future Commitments*[3] (PRESENT VALUE)		Column IV CAMPAIGN TOTAL Column I plus II	Column V CAMPAIGN TOTAL Column I plus III
	Featured Objectives	Other Objectives	Featured Objectives	Other Objectives	Featured Objectives	Other Objectives		
A. Alumni	$	$	$	$	$	$	$	$
B. Parents								
C. Other Individuals								
D. Foundations								
E. Corporations								
F. Religious Organizations								
G. Consortia								
H. Other								
TOTAL								

[1] Outright commitments to be paid during the campaign period and the pledge-payment period.
[2] Face value of deferred commitments received during the campaign period for which a specific maturation date cannot be determined.
[3] Present value of deferred commitments received during the campaign period for which a specific maturation date cannot be determined.

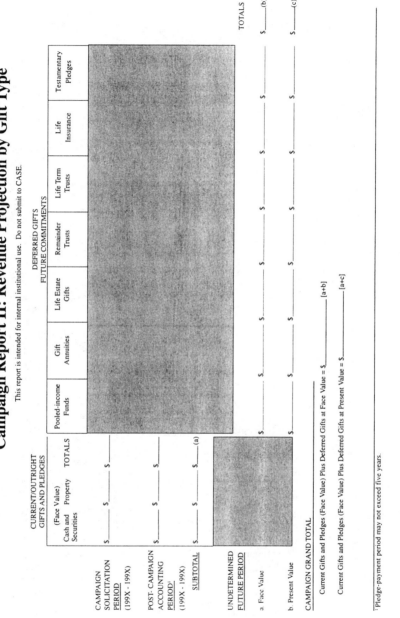

Campaign Report II: Revenue Projection by Gift Type

This report is intended for internal institutional use. Do not submit to CASE.

	CURRENT/OUTRIGHT GIFTS AND PLEDGES			DEFERRED GIFTS FUTURE COMMITMENTS							
	(Face Value) Cash and Securities	Property	TOTALS	Pooled-income Funds	Gift Annuities	Life Estate Gifts	Remainder Trusts	Life Term Trusts	Life Insurance	Testamentary Pledges	TOTALS
CAMPAIGN SOLICITATION PERIOD (199X - 199X)	$ ____	$ ____	$ ____								
POST-CAMPAIGN ACCOUNTING PERIOD¹ (199X - 199X)	$ ____	$ ____	$ ____								
SUBTOTAL	$ ____	$ ____ (a)		$ ____	$ ____	$ ____	$ ____	$ ____	$ ____	$ ____ (b)	
UNDETERMINED FUTURE PERIOD				$ ____	$ ____	$ ____	$ ____	$ ____	$ ____	$ ____ (c)	

CAMPAIGN GRAND TOTAL

Current Gifts and Pledges (Face Value) Plus Deferred Gifts at Face Value = $ _____ [a+b]

Current Gifts and Pledges (Face Value) Plus Deferred Gifts at Present Value = $ _____ [a+c]

a. Face Value

b. Present Value

¹ Pledge-payment period may not exceed five years.

Present-value Calculation:
Background and Methodology

CONCEPTUAL BACKGROUND

The financial world recognizes today's value of an asset that will not be realized until some time in the future through the mechanism of present value discounting. The present value of a future interest is nothing more than a statement of what the future amount would be worth in terms of today's dollar value.

In the case of deferred gifts such as bequests and life insurance, where the value of the amount received by the institution is measured merely by the passage of time, its present value is a function of the donor or insured's actuarial life expectancy and an assumed interest rate at which the amount is discounted. In turn, the assumed rate at which the amount is discounted is generally a function of the earning power of assets in the economy when the donor makes the gift (or the commitment, in the case of a bequest). These standards use the widely publicized *Applicable Federal Rate* (AFR) as the discount factor.

In the case of deferred gifts such as charitable remainder trusts and pooled-income funds, the additional factors of (1) the amount to be paid to the beneficiary(ies) over the term of the trust or the life expectancy(ies) of the beneficiary(ies), and (2) the number of beneficiaries also figure into the present-value calculation.

In the case of a stream of payments such as the lead-trust income to be paid to an institution or a gift annuity to an annuitant, the present value of the income stream is the current equivalent in terms of a lump sum value that the recipient will receive over time.

The *Internal Revenue Code* allows donors to claim income tax charitable deductions equal to today's value of money or assets donated for charitable purposes, subject to any limitations provided in the tax laws. Where the gift is currently given for immediate use with no return benefit to the donor, the current full fair-market value is the amount available for the deduction. Where a return benefit is given to the donor or where the institution cannot currently have complete access to the transferred amount, such as in a charitable remainder trust, the value will be less than full fair-market value.

Where an amount allowable as a charitable deduction is less than fair-market value, the *Internal Revenue Code* requires that the Applicable Federal Rate be used to determine its present value. This rate is released by the U.S. Department of the Treasury each month. It can be found in the *Wall Street Journal* approximately the 22nd to 24th day of each month. The AFR may also be found in the *Chronicle of Philanthropy*, several newsletters, and in mailings from various software vendors.

The Income Tax Act of Canada does not allow a charitable deduction for money or assets donated for charitable purposes. Instead, it allows a two-tiered tax credit for such gifts. Nevertheless, for purposes of these reporting standards, a present value of a future interest is necessary. The institution's accountant or actuary may perform this calculation or a computer-generated present value may also be used. For institutions in the United States, credit for deferred gifts to a campaign should be the same as the amount allowable as a deduction by the IRS, *before* limits on the deduction that pertain specifically to the donor in question, such as reductions and percentage limitations. Tax laws and regulations of the United States and of Canada should be consulted for specifics.

Life Expectancy Tables, Ages 25-90

(Table V—Ordinary Life Annuities; One Life—Expected Return Multiples)

AGE	MULTIPLE	AGE	MULTIPLE	AGE	MULTIPLE	AGE	MULTIPLE
25	57.9	40	42.5	58	25.9	75	12.5
26	56.0	41	41.5	59	25.0	76	11.9
27	55.1	42	40.6	60	24.2	77	11.2
28	54.1	43	39.6	61	23.3	78	10.6
29	53.1	44	38.7	62	22.5	79	10.0
30	52.2	45	37.7	63	21.6	80	9.5
31	51.2	46	36.8	64	20.8	81	8.9
32	50.2	47	35.9	65	20.0	82	8.4
33	49.3	48	34.9	66	19.2	83	7.9
34	48.3	49	34.0	67	18.4	84	7.4
35	47.3	50	33.1	68	17.6	85	6.9
36	46.4	51	32.2	69	16.8	86	6.5
37	45.4	52	31.3	70	16.0	87	6.1
38	44.4	53	30.4	71	15.3	88	5.7
39	43.5	54	29.5	72	14.6	89	5.3
		55	28.6	73	13.9	90	5.0
		56	27.7	74	13.2		
		57	26.8				

Source: IRS § Reg. 1.72.9, 1993.

Sample Deferred Pledge Agreement

In consideration of my interest in education, for and in consideration of the similar promises of other donors and for other good and valuable consideration, the receipt of which is hereby acknowledged, and intending to be legally bound, I, [DONOR'S NAME], irrevocably pledge and promise that [IN THE EVENT THAT MY SPOUSE (SPOUSE'S NAME) PREDECEASES ME] my estate shall be obligated to pay [NAME OF INSTITUTION], subsequent to my death, the sum of [NUMBER AND 00/100 DOLLARS] .

This sum, when paid from my estate, shall be used by [NAME OF INSTITUTION] for the [SPECIFY NAME OF SCHOLARSHIP, FUND, PROJECT, ETC.].

I direct my executor, administrator, trustee, or other personal representative to pay this sum within one (1) year from the date of my death, without interest if paid within such period.

I acknowledge that [NAME OF INSTITUTION'S] promise to use the amount pledged by me and/or that [NAME OF INSTITUTION'S] actual use of the money pledged by me for the purposes specified shall each constitute full and adequate consideration for this pledge.

This pledge is to be irrevocable and a binding obligation upon my estate.

Lifetime payments may satisfy pledge. This Deferred Pledge Agreement may also be satisfied in part or in full by payments made by [MY SPOUSE OR] me at my [OUR] discretion during my [OUR] lifetime[s] and so designated by [MY SPOUSE OR] me in writing delivered to [NAME OF INSTITUTION] at the time of the gift. Any amounts paid by [MY SPOUSE OR] me from the date of this Agreement to the date of my death which are so designated shall reduce the amount my estate is obligated to pay after my death under the terms of this Agreement. Any amounts not so designated shall conclusively be presumed not to be in reduction of the amount pledged herein.

Gifts by will or living trust reduce pledge. In the event that [NAME OF INSTITUTION] is a beneficiary under the terms of my duly probated Will or Living Trust, whether a specific or residuary legatee, the amount received by [NAME OF INSTITUTION] under the terms of my Will or Living Trust shall reduce the amount pledged in this Agreement.

This agreement shall be interpreted under the laws of [SPECIFY STATE].

EXECUTED THIS _____ day of _____, 19_____.

DONOR:

_____   _____
[Donor's Name]   [Donor's Signature]

WITNESS:

_____   _____
[Witness's Name]   [Witness's Signature]

20
_____

ACCEPTANCE

The undersigned, being a duly authorized officer of [NAME OF INSTITUTION], does hereby accept the within pledge.

UNIVERSITY OFFICER:

_____   _____
[Officer's Name]   [Officer's Signature]

Appendix G

21

Sample Contract to Make a Will

THIS AGREEMENT is made this _____ day of _____, 19___, by and between [DONOR'S NAME] of [CITY, STATE] (hereinafter referred to as "the Donor")

-AND-

[NAME OF INSTITUTION] of [CITY, STATE] (hereinafter referred to as "the Institution").

RECITALS

A. [NAME OF INSTITUTION] is an educational institution and, in such capacity, renders a variety of programs and services in the field of education.

B. Donor, in furtherance of [NAME OF INSTITUTION]'s programs and services, and as an incentive to others to contribute to [NAME OF INSTITUTION], desires to commit, promise, and pledge to [NAME OF INSTITUTION] [SPECIFY PERCENT (__%)] percent of the residue of [HIS/HER] estate as hereinafter defined.

C. Donor wishes to have [HIS/HER] commitment as set forth in this document be irrevocable by virtue of this agreement, in order to insure that [HIS/HER] testamentary gift to [NAME OF INSTITUTION] can be treated as a current gift to [NAME OF INSTITUTION] for purposes of [NAME OF INSTITUTION]'s procedures.

D. [NAME OF INSTITUTION] and the Donor wish to have their complete agreement in this regard set forth in this document.

NOW, THEREFORE, for good and valuable consideration, the receipt of which is hereby acknowledged by each party, the parties to this Agreement, intending to be legally bound, pledge, covenant, and agree as follows:

1. *Testamentary Gift.* Donor irrevocably pledges and agrees that [HE/SHE] has executed or immediately will execute a valid Will or Living Trust which shall provide that [SPECIFY PERCENT (___%)] percent of the residue of [HIS/HER] estate (as that phrase is defined in Paragraph 3 of this Agreement) shall pass outright to [NAME OF INSTITUTION] to be used for [STATE PURPOSE].

2. *Use by [NAME OF INSTITUTION].* [NAME OF INSTITUTION] hereby agrees to utilize the amount received for the purpose and in the manner described in Paragraph 1 above.

3. *Definition of "Residue of the Estate."* The phrase "Residue of the Estate" as it is used in this Agreement shall mean all property (real, personal, and mixed) owned by Donor individually, less any debts, funeral and other last expenses, administrative expenses, and applicable death taxes; provided, however, that the Donor shall have the right to make the following specific bequests:

22

_____

[ITEMIZE ALL SPECIFIC BEQUESTS]

4. *Estimate of Worth.* The Donor represents to [NAME OF INSTITUTION] that, if the provisions of Paragraph 1 of this Agreement were to become operative as of the date of this Agreement, the value of [SPECIFY PERCENT (___%)] percent of the residue of the estate passing to [NAME OF INSTITUTION] would approximate [SPECIFY AMOUNT AND 00/100 ($)] dollars.

5. *Provision Not to be Revoked or Amended.* The Donor agrees that any Will, Living Trust, or beneficiary designation subsequently executed in replacement of those referred to in Paragraph 1 of this Agreement shall dispose of the residue of the estate in the same manner as provided in Paragraph 1 of this Agreement. Donor further agrees that [HE/SHE] shall not execute a Codicil to the Will or an amendment to the Living Trust provided for in Paragraph 1 of this Agreement which would have the effect of partially or fully eliminating or modifying dispositions of the residue of the estate provided for in Paragraph 1 of this Agreement.

6. *Power to Rescind or Amend.* The parties to this Agreement reserve the power to jointly rescind or amend this Agreement by written agreement signed by each of them to such effect.

7. *Heirs and Assigns.* This Agreement shall be binding upon the successors, heirs, personal representative, and assigns of each party.

8. *Governing Law.* This Agreement shall be interpreted in accordance with the laws of the [SPECIFY STATE OR PROVINCE].

EXECUTED the day and year first above written.

WITNESS: DONOR:

_____   _____
[Witness's Signature]   [Donor's Signature]

[NAME OF INSTITUTION]

_____   By:_____
[Attest]   [Authorized Signature]

About the Author

G. David Gearhart is senior vice president for development and university relations at The Pennsylvania State University. Since he joined the university in 1985 as vice president for development and university relations, the Division of Development and University Relations has been awarded the Grand Gold Medal by the Council for Advancement and Support of Education in 1987, 1988, and 1991. This award recognizes the best institutional advancement program in the nation. Dr. Gearhart was appointed senior vice president in 1988.

Dr. Gearhart began his career in higher education in 1976 as assistant to the president at Westminster College. He has served in a variety of capacities at several institutions, including director of development at Westminster and the Winston Churchill Memorial and Library, vice president of Hendrix College, and director of development of the University of Arkansas.

Dr. Gearhart is a member of the American Bar Association. In 1991, he was named a Fulbright Scholar and studied at Oxford University. He received his undergraduate degree at Westminster College and a law degree and a doctor of education degree from the University of Arkansas.